subscribe

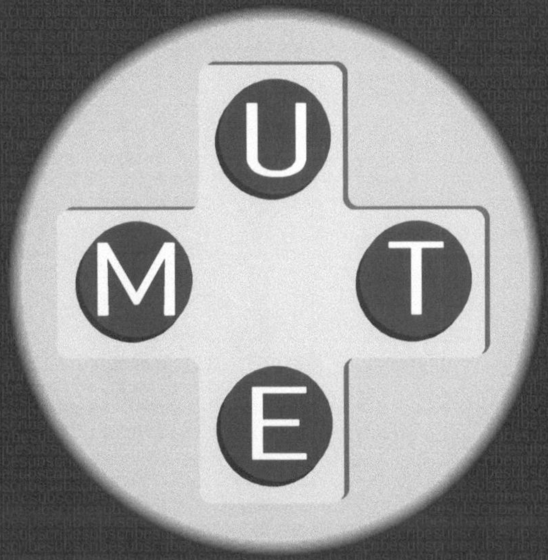

Tel +44 (0)171 613 4743
Fax +44 (0)171 613 4052
e-mail subs@metamute.com
web www.metamute.com/subs

Do not underestimate the power of foreplay

Electronic Arts at Middlesex University

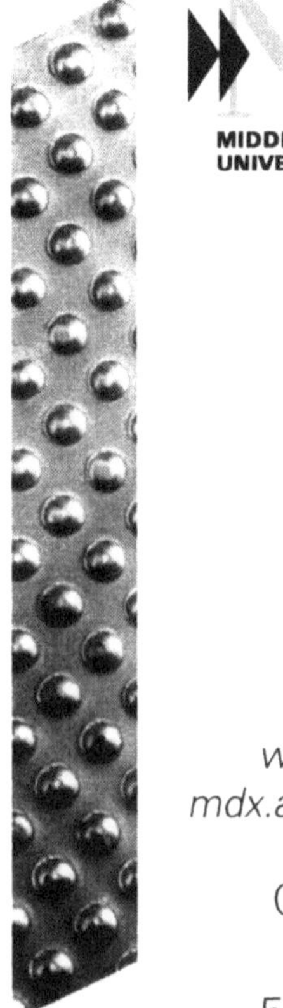

MIDDLESEX UNIVERSITY

- **BA Honours Sonic Arts**
  Three years full-time
  Electroacoustic music, audio computing, sound synthesis, MIDI programming, digital audition, psychoacoustics, interactive composition, sound in multimedia, etc
- **MA Digital Arts**
  One year full-time or two years part-time
- **MA Electronic Arts**
  One year full-time or two years part-time
- **MA Design for Interactive Media**
  One year full-time
- **MA Video**
  One year full-time
- **Centre for Electronic Arts**
  Research opportunities

www. mdx.ac.uk

0181 362 5898

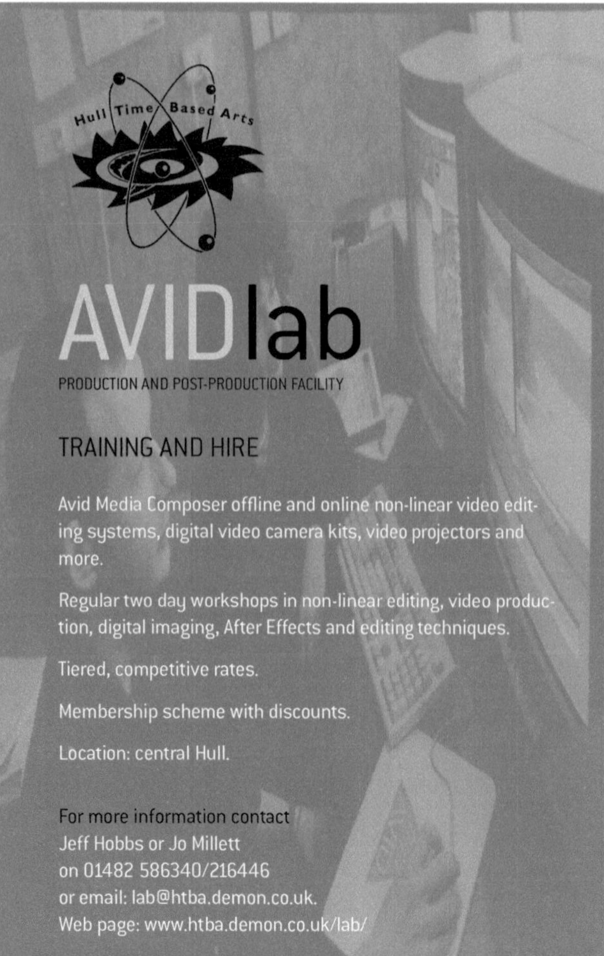

@MUTE

EDITORS
Pauline van Mourik Broekman and Simon Worthington
ASSISTANT EDITOR Josephine Berry

EDITORIAL TEAM/SECTION EDITORS
AUDIOPHILE Hari Kunzru
READ ME Jamie King and Tom McCarthy
GAMING John Paul Bichard
DEEP BLUE James Flint
SHORT/CUTS, ART TM & SHELF LIFE Mute editorial team
OUR MAN IN HAVANA Micz Flor
TYPOGRAPHY AND DESIGN Damian Jaques ('Mr. Pleasure')
CREATIVE DIRECTORS SW & PvMB
WEB DESIGN Tina Spear and Micz Flor
SUPERINTERN Alison Bell
With special thanks to Lee Dradpour and Bibliotech
PUBLISHER Skyscraper Digital Publishing

EDITORIAL
Mute, 2nd floor, 135–139 Curtain Road, London EC2A 3BX, UK
T +44 (0)171 613 4743 F +44 (0)171 613 4052
e-mail: mute@metamute.com web: www.metamute.com
WEB SERVICES Lovely: www.lovely.net

ADVERTISING
Ben Mayers, Applejack, 24 St. Lukes Mews, London, W11 1DF, UK
T +44 (0)171 221 8199 F +44 (0)171 221 8175
e-mail: bmayers@dircon.co.uk

DISTRIBUTION
UK*
Time Out Distribution,
Universal House, 251 Tottenham Road, London, W1P 0AB.
T +44 (0)171 813 6060 F +44 (0)171 813 6039
Central Books,
99 Wallis Road, London, E4 5LN.
T +44 (0)181 986 4854 F +44 (0)181 533 5821
*See also cybercafe listings (p.72) for regional Mute outlets
USA
Desert Moon Periodicals/Xines,
1226 Calle de Comercio, Santa Fe, NM 87505, USA.
T +1 (0)505 474 6311 F +1 (0)505 474 6317
e-mail: xines@nets.com web: www.swcp.com/xines/homepage.htm
Total Circulation Services,
Inc., 80 Fredrick Street, Hackensack, N.J. 07601, USA.
T +1 (0)201 342 6334 F +1 (0)201 342 2756
CANADA
Speedimpex,
Unit 1, 155 Deerhide Crescent, Weston, Ontario, Canada M9M 2Z2.
T +1 (0)416 741 7555 F +1 (0)416 741 4634
NEW ZEALAND
Propaganda Distributors,
No. 2 Carr Road, Mt. Roskill, Aukland, New Zealand.
T (0)9 625 3000 F (0)9 625 3030
email: prop@gordongotch.co.nz
AUSTRALIA
Multipoint Distribution,
PO Box 86, Eastern Mail Centre, Vic 3110, Australia.
T +61 (0)3 9872 6314 F +61 (0)3 9720 9177

SUBSCRIPTION RATES
uk/eu: individual £10, institutional/corporate £20, 1 year/4 issues
other: individual £18/$27, institutional/corporate £28/$42, 1 year/4 issues
Mute single and back issues:
£4/$6 inc. p&p, Pilot & Issue 1,2,3,4,5,6,7,8 available.
The BAC PACK offers a chance to collect a special edition of boxed back issues.
Year 1: pilot,1,2,3 (94/95) uk/eu £14, other £18/$27
Year 2: 4,5,6,7 (96-97) uk/eu £14, other £18/$27
Payment Methods: visa/master card/uk cheque/uk postal-order.
e-mail: subs@metamute.com

SPECIAL THANKS TO Imogen O'Rorke – Head Rabbit, Francesca Barnes, Tina Spear & Daniel Jackson, Justin Greetham, Tallboy & Stephen da Silva, Suzanne and Lloyd at Bibliotech, Steven Brown Associates, the Bean (& Emma the Mute pin-up) and all our contributors, of past and current issues. Mute also wishes to thank The East London Partnership and SBC Warburg for their support.

FONTS
Headers are set in Udo (der Disco Konig) by Fountain Fonts [www.algonet.se/~fountain]
Body typeset in ITC Century Light Condensed and ITC Conduit Light [www.itcfonts.com]
Mute title set in Mutelitterman ©mute thanks to Maxine Grigson

The views expressed in Mute and Metamute are not necessarily those of the publishers or service providers. All rights reserved. © All material copyright the authors and Mute 1998.

Mute is published in the U.K. by Skyscraper Digital Publishing and printed at CBC Print Ltd., Luton. Film outputting Bibliotech, Hoxton, London. ISSN 1356-7748

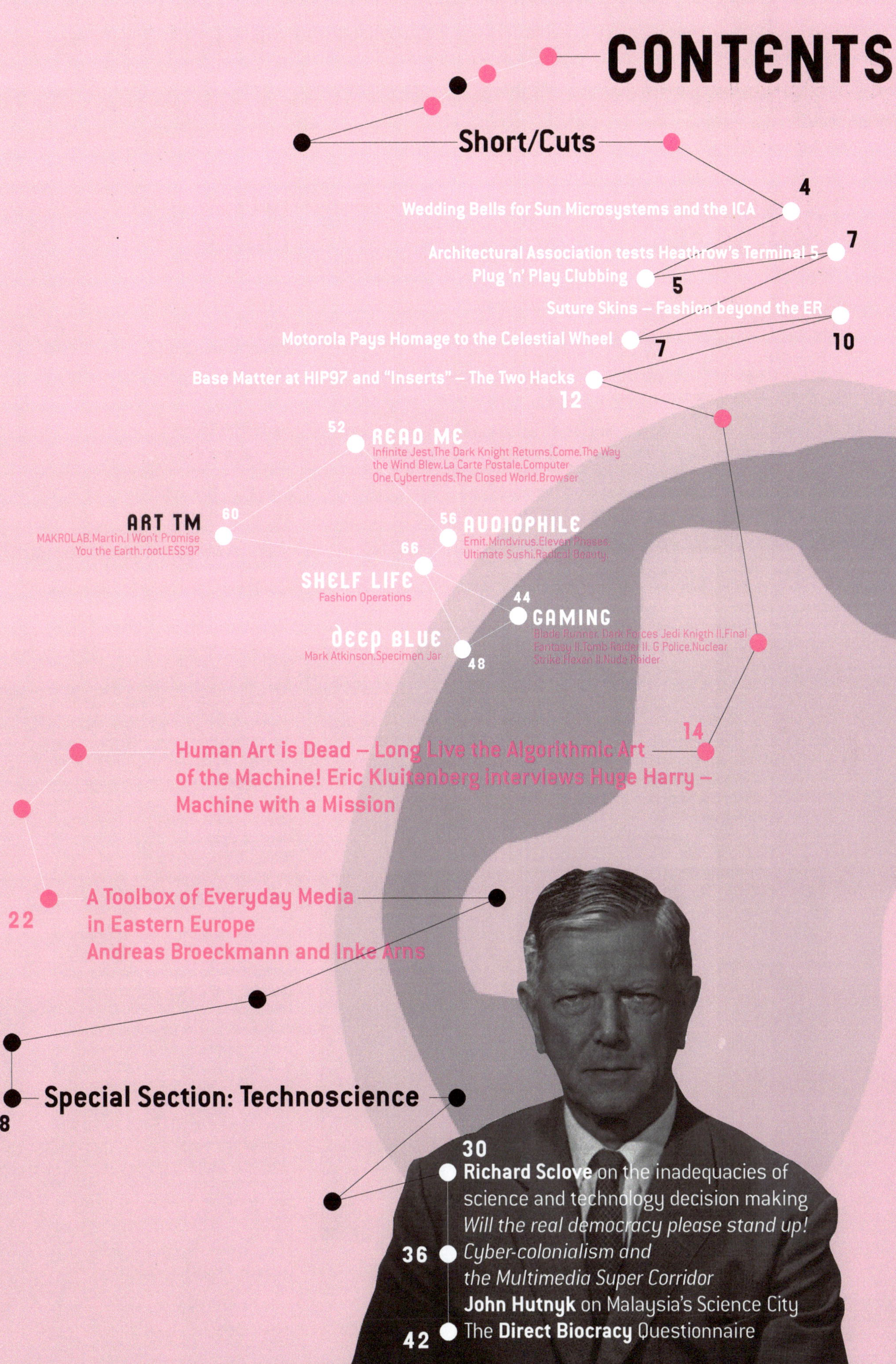

CONTENTS

NEWMEDIA CENTRE.COY

Judging by the fanfare, the recent marriage between Sun Microsystems and London's Institute of Contemporary Art was a match made in heaven. Reportedly the outcome of months of negotiations, the partners' mutual suitability has enjoyed the kind of scrutiny you can only expect from the best arranged marriages. Yet, a few months after the euphoric pronouncements of November's opening, in which Sun presented its new 'digital playground', the ICA its 'collaboration of equals' and the New Labour Government its support of the 'creative industries', clues revealing who's wearing the trousers are there for all to see.

Essentially, the fuss is focused on 2 million pounds worth of 'kit' (as the with-it PR team put it). This figure, plus the Sun workstations and miscellaneous gear that it bought the centre, are banded about as proof of Sun's serious commitment to cultural experimentation.

But what, seriously, is £2m in a year's budget of a company like Sun when it receives such goodies in exchange as a corporate training and hospitality venue on the Mall, a 'radical' image, and no doubt a favourable impression in the oh so technologically-minded UK government? More importantly, what use is £2m worth of kit to a creative set-up where consistent technical assistance is as lacking as it seems to be at newmediacentre.com? Little thought has been given to the disparities between existing levels of knowledge among artists and that needed to make the work the 'kit' is capable of. To pay the deal its dues in the favoured parlance: "Man, it's just so top-down!"

Most illuminating is the website; corporate platforms don't come much more transparent than this. "Sun wants to support those who are creating the future – the innovators who challenge today's status quo and help shape tomorrow's world". Yeah, yeah. Its anodyne and ill-informed copy is a textbook example of the kind of prescriptive take on technology many artists using computers are trying to challenge. Ploddingly slow, and badly structured, it also commits the corporate 'sin' of being user-unfriendly. It's early days, but if 'nurturing creativity' means writing glossaries and absolutist definitions of new media, it really begs the question whether Sun *or* the ICA knows its spouse at all!

[www.newmediacentre.com]

PvMB

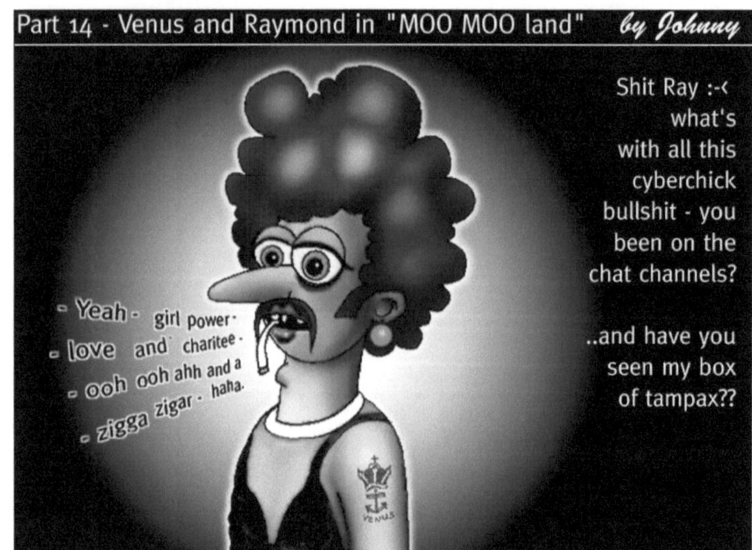

LITTLE and LARGE

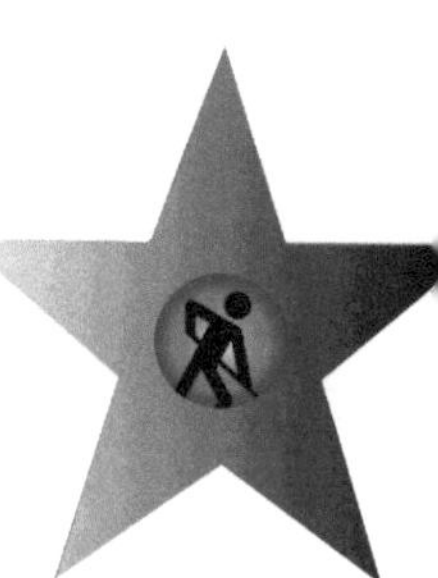

Media Independents Open Talks with Governments and Industry

by Amendsen Scott

At Amsterdam's 'From Practice to Policy' conference this October, representatives from 22 European organisations working with media culture gathered with policy makers, educationalists and industrialists to debate the principles of a European media policy. This ambitious undertaking was initiated by a Dutch association of media organisations called The Virtual Platform and centred on 'The Amsterdam Agenda'. This is a collaborative document, resulting from a series of private discussions between media practitioners and then debated publicly at the conference, which sets out shared characteristics of independent media activity. These, they argue, are crucial to the critical and creative development of ICT and its use across Europe. The Agenda advocates a closer collaboration between independent media groups, industry and governments. The nitty gritty of the document comes at its end, after a quite lengthy paean to creative media practice, with a list of practical proposals. Amongst others, they suggest making free access to public media an objective of cultural policies, supporting networks of specialised and small institutions, making available small-scale project funding and above all stress the priority of making investment in people over technology. The David-and-Goliath-like feat of these small independent organisations taking on international power brokers is truly awe inspiring and, although the real effects of P2P are still unknown, its message to independent users is clear: either start dealing with the powers that be or surrender the web to the voracious forces of the free market.

[www.dds.nl/p2p]

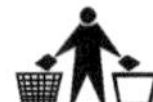

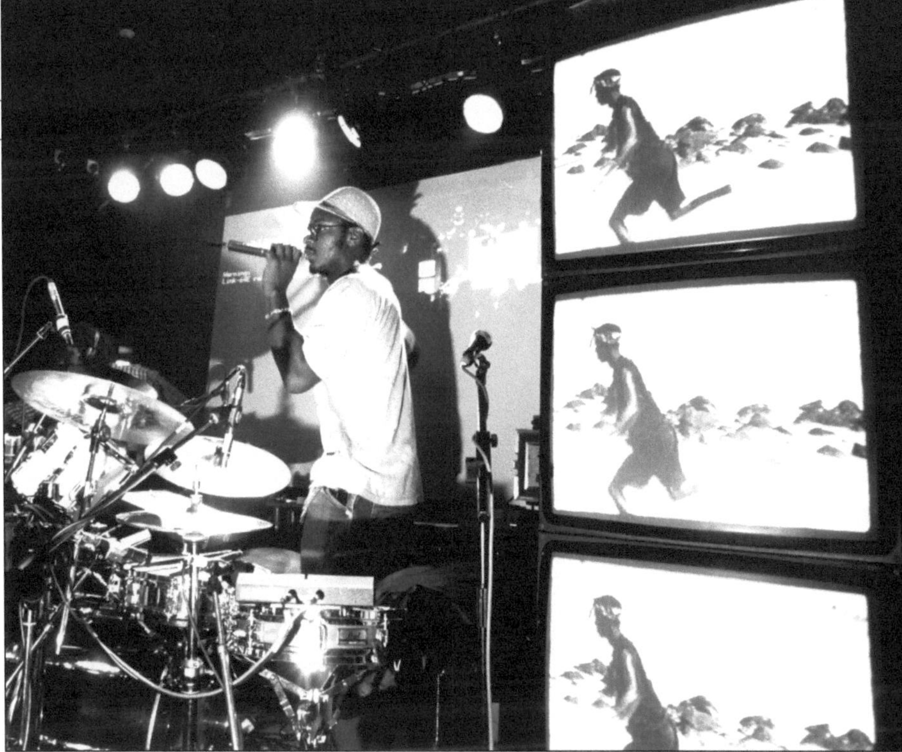

THE PLUG 'N' PLAY CLUB

by James Flint

Standing in the crowd at the recent Hyperjam event in East London's The Vibe Bar, it seemed that the 'interactive club' was finally coming of age. The night, organised by Derek Richards to celebrate the Irish festival of Samhain, featured an ISDN link-up between Cleveland Watkiss and Project 23 in London and percussionist Talvin Singh and the Afrocelts Sound System in Dublin. With two wall-sized screen projections, an excellent PA and clever use of lighting, the Hyperjam organisers managed to create that most elusive of things in a digitally enhanced space – atmosphere.

Although not involved in the Hyperjam event, one of the people most responsible for hacking this combination of performance and technology into a form malleable enough to be effective as a format is Marc Boothe. Marc's organisation Digital Diaspora has been putting on link-ups for over two years, from a New York – London call and response link-up featuring Tony Remy, Cut Master Swift and D.J. Spooky at the ICA in April 1995 to two nights at this year's Camden Mix, in which Afrika Bambaataa, LTJ Bukem and A Guy called Gerald were all involved.

Marc's aim has never been to simply insert technology into a traditional club, but to reinvent the clubbing experience around the technology. To this end he has recruited not just DJs and musicians to his cause (he has already worked with the likes of Steve Williamson, Marque Gilmore, Grooverider and Vernon Reid), but also poets, writers and video makers. Bringing all these people together, first in 'digital playground' sessions, where they can meet and fool around with the technology, and later in the link-ups – or 'slams' – themselves, has meant that Digital Diaspora events have taken shape in an organic manner. The result of this is that the artists involved are comfortable with the technology (which tends to actually work at a DD slam, an achievement in itself) and can concentrate on the job in hand. "This means you get a proper performance," according to Marc, "and not just a 'Yo, London! Yo, New York!' We've been there, done that." (The Camden Mix events were also broadcast live on the DD website [www.diaspora.co.uk].)

One of the problems with a slam-style event is that an audience is not always sure what they're meant to get into. Are you supposed to focus on the local end of the link-up, or what's coming down the line? Are you supposed to watch the screen or the stage? The fact that everyone's attention is constantly shifting means it's difficult for a mood or atmosphere to coalesce. Marc agrees that "essentially you're leading the audience down a path with no rails." The DD solution to the problem has been to use as many live artists as possible, although this brings problems of its own, since you need to make sure that there aren't time lags between the performers (say a guitarist in New York and a drummer in London) of more than 80 milliseconds – much harder when you're dealing with transatlantic distances than when you're trying to do link-ups within Europe. Does this mean then that ISDN is all set to spearhead a live music in clubs revival? It doesn't seem like it's beyond the bounds of possibility.

Xjim@metamute.com**X**

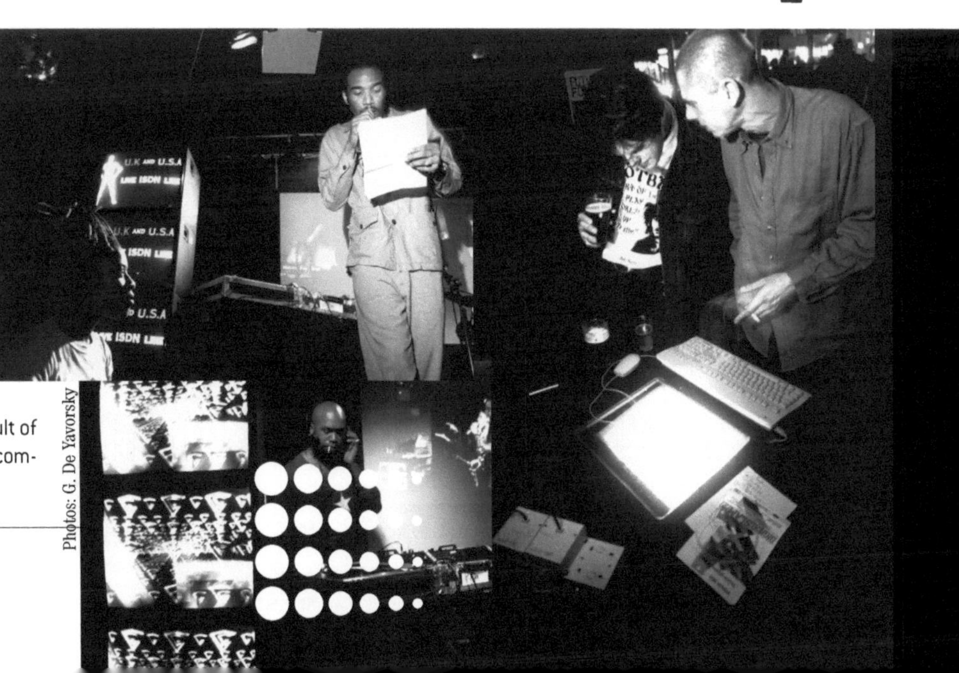

Photos: G. De Yavorsky

SWOOSH – YOU ARE NOW ENTERING AIR SPACE

by Josephine Berry

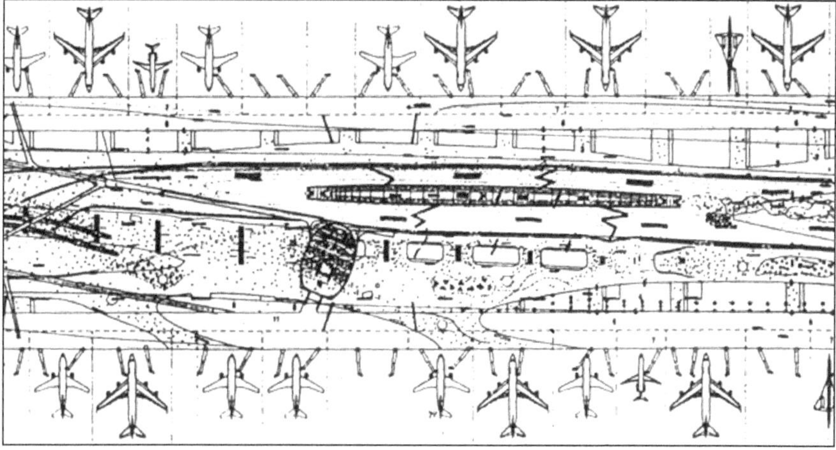

Imagine you're walking fast with all your senses concentrated on avoiding the pedestrians moving towards you, accelerating sometimes when you see a chance to overtake the person in front, then slowing down to avoid colliding with someone else who's stopped to check their orientation. Your eyes flit constantly across the window displays in the strings of high street shops and, whilst making complicated calculations involving desire, requirement and finance, your nostrils are filled with the smells of baking pizzas and cooking coffee, you post a letter, watch lovers embrace, someone getting arrested, meet friends at a rendezvous, read the headlines on a bundle of newspapers...

Once this passage would only have described movement through an urban space, now it can also fit to the experiences we have in a single building – just think 'airport'. Designing airports has become one of the architect's most concerted logistical nightmares – probably because they need to solve urban scale problems within building scale parameters. What better project then to set MA students at the Architectural Association than this – especially in light of the wholly uninspiring design produced by Richard Rogers' practice for Heathrow Terminal 5, currently under construction.

Brett Steele and Patrik Schumacher of the AA's Design Research Laboratory developed the 'Heathrow Experiment' project for their students because, they believe, the airport's 'complexity' and 'hybridity' have become some of postmodernity's defining characteristics. These conditions demand that instead of transferring traditional models of urban-

Visual Arts Grants 1998/99

The Visual Arts Department aims to extend the understanding and appreciation of the visual arts and to support a range of contemporary practice. The department is inviting applications for funding for projects taking place in England in 1998/99 under the following schemes:

Scheme	Deadline
Artists in Sites for Learning	12/01/98
Artists Film & Video National Fund: Exhibitions & Initiatives	03/02/98 & 01/10/98
Exhibition Production	09/02/98
Media Publications: Photography, Film & Video and Digital Media	23/02/98
Symposia	25/02/98
Artists' First Time Publications	25/02/98
Architecture	02/03/98
Exhibition Research & Development	01/04/98

Whilst we welcome applications from artists' groups and artist-run organisations, individual artists wishing to develop or promote their own work are not eligible to apply under these schemes.

For further details, please send an A5 SAE to the Visual Arts Department, Arts Council of England, 14 Great Peter Street, London SW1P 3NQ, indicating in which awards you are interested. You can telephone us on 0171 333 0100, fax us on 0171 973 6590 or e-mail: info.visualart.ace@artsfb.org.uk

The Arts Council is committed to an equal opportunities policy.

THE **ARTS COUNCIL** OF ENGLAND

LEA Gallery

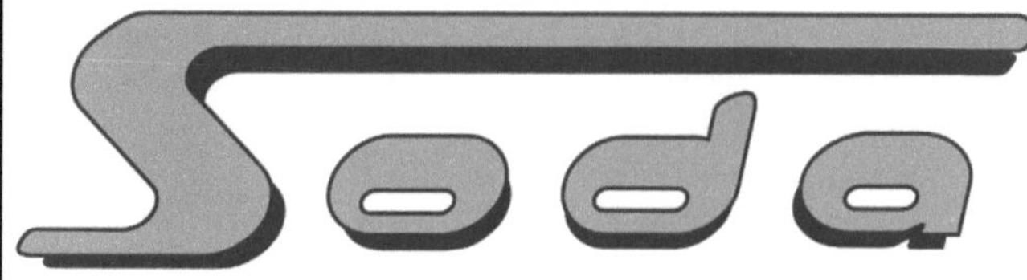

Night time window projections GARY HUME

16 January - 27 February 1998

Wednesday - Friday 12 - 7
Saturday - Sunday 12 - 6

The Lux Centre, 2-4 Hoxton Square, London N1 6NU
Tel: 0171 684 0101 E-mail: lea@easynet.co.uk
http://www.lea.org.uk
Nearest tube: Old Street

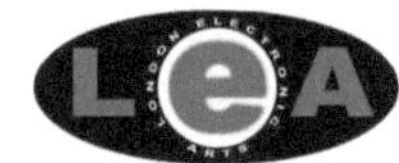

Presented by London Electronic Arts with the support of the London Film and Video Development Agency and the Arts Council of England

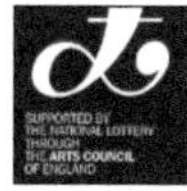

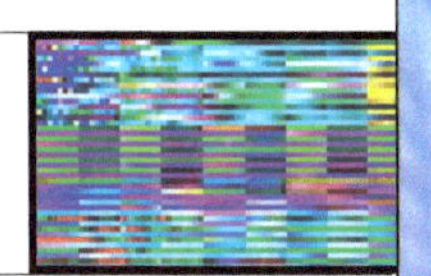

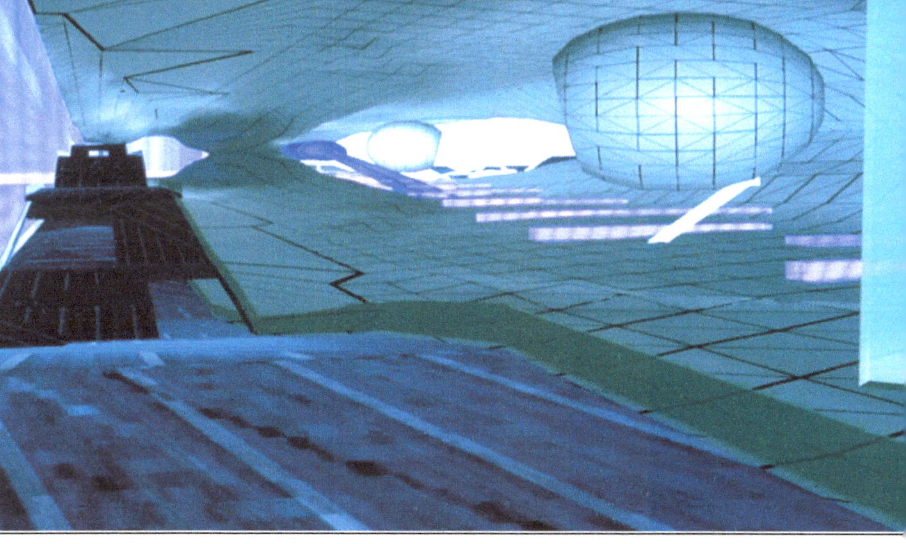

ism à la Richard Rogers, "new synthetic worlds be imagined". This previous model, they insist, cannot accommodate the "logic of these massive infrastructure nodes" nor "integrate a multiplicity of programmes". In what Schumacher describes as a post-Fordist world, where 'flexibility' and 'multi-task orientation' have become keywords, the old fashioned city is just too rigid and segmented a model to continue to be useful. The "programmatic reality" of 700 seater restaurants, the en masse art viewing experience of the new Bankside Tate Gallery, the massive continuous interiors of shopping malls etc. have, they contend, established new types of 'synthetic urbanism' that can actually learn from the airport model.

In recent history, airports have been the object of intense critical scrutiny. At the 'Airport' conference at the AA this October, the artist Martha Rosler showed a series of her slides taken in international airports. These images underscore the prevalent view that airports have come to epitomise the phenomenon of 'non-place'. Her photographs mix generic advertising images and messages with lone figures of lost looking travellers and despondent staff, in a condemnation of the airport's substitution of real for simulated experience. Schumacher and Steele are quick to reject this trend in theory. Steele describes the airport as, "a place where the set of characteristics are so fundamentally different that it doesn't need to be thought of as the denial of something that is already known. It's a lived condition that's real today, that demands its own attention on its own terms." Far from the airport being a derivative simulation of the real city then, it provides an authentic alternative to an outdated traditional urbanism that can no longer accommodate our new found hybridity. Just another crock of PoMo BS? Ask yourself that question next time you're at the cashpoint, scanning the Costa Coffee range, soaking up advertising slogans, listening to your Walkman and feeling the ecstatic vibrations of your pocket pager.

Xjosie@metamute.com**X**

THE 77TH ELEMENT

by Simon Worthington

The Iridium® project is a belt of 77 satellites circling the earth at a range of 780km. At a cost of $4 billion Iridium® will provide a communications network that can handle voice-, fax-, data- or pager-signals to reach any destination on earth. Initiated by a conglomerate of 17 investor-organisations headed by communications giant Motorola, it is due to become active in September 1998.

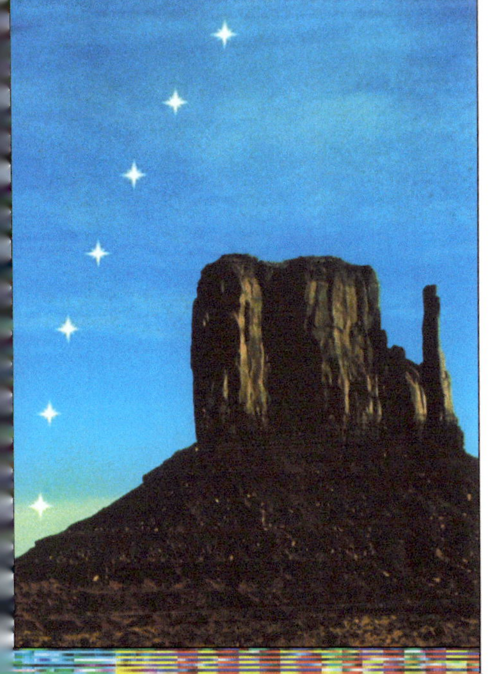

But Iridium® is *more* than a globe shrinking communications network. Iridium® is ART! Little known to its new supervisors, it bears an uncanny resemblance to the space-art project *Celestial Wheel* proposed by artist Jean Marc Philippe in the early seventies (1970-1972). *Celestial Wheel* was to encircle the earth with a corona of orbiting satellites carrying small lasers that would be visible from earth. The string of Iridium® satellites – each carrying a 3 pronged antenna – reflect the sun's rays and, in optimum conditions, can even be seen in the daytime. By mid 1998 this new-variant *Celestial Wheel* will be a reality.

Philippe's original was to create a circle of light visible high in the sky at the equator, moving further toward the horizon depending on your proximity to the poles. Due to its enormous scale, Philippe mused, the ring of satellites could also make the speed of light perceptible – its 0.9 second orbit made visible by literally illuminating the lasers at the required intervals.

As there is a thin line between exhibiting sponsored artwork and advertising, the US Congressional ban on advertising in space presents a serious obstacle to art-in-space. As with Iridium®

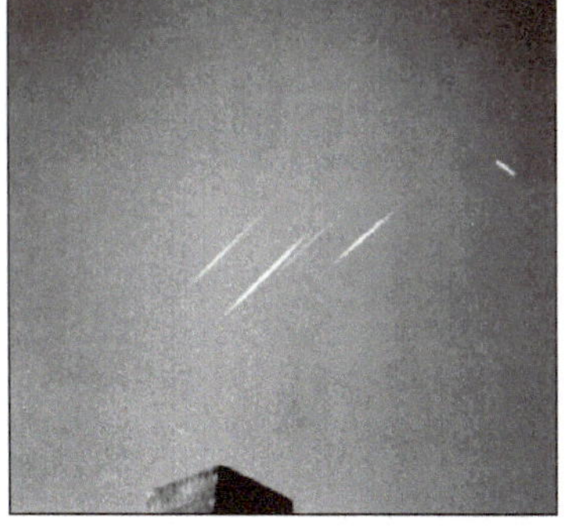

we'll have to be happy with 'Space Capital' spin-offs or with objects in space such as the 1969 artwork *The Moon Museum*, a small ceramic tile carried on Apollo 12 on which, amongst others, Robert Rauschenberg drew a straight line and Andy Warhol a penis.

Xsimon@metamute.com**X**

[www.iridium.com]
[www.spaceart.net]

Left: Jean-Marc Philippe, *Celestial Wheel*, 1970-1972, from Frank Popper, *Art of the Electronic Age*, Harry N. Abrams, Inc. 1993
Right: Iridium satellite, 1997
© Paul Maley mtempleman@us.superscape.com

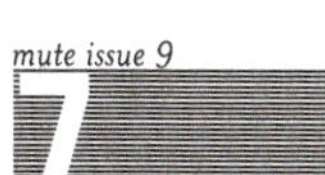

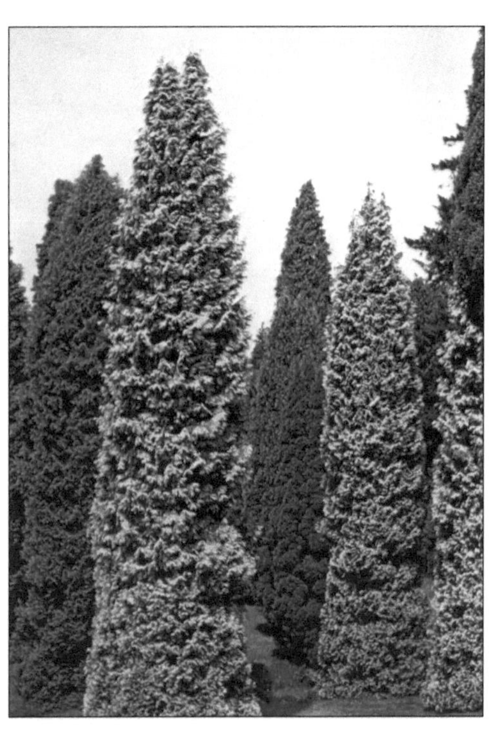

HOW YOU COME TO TERMS WITH
THE GODDESS
IS NO CONCERN OF MINE

Pictures of Lily Catalogues are available from Jeremy Akerman @ 63 Scylla Road, London, SE15 3PR. £6 p&p inc. Collage for *Mute* magazine, Jeremy Akerman and Michael Curran. Images collection J. Akerman, M. Curran and Tariq Alvi.

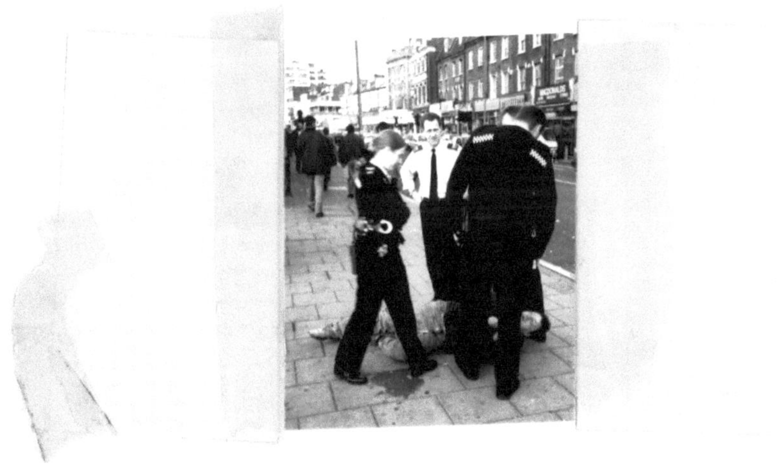

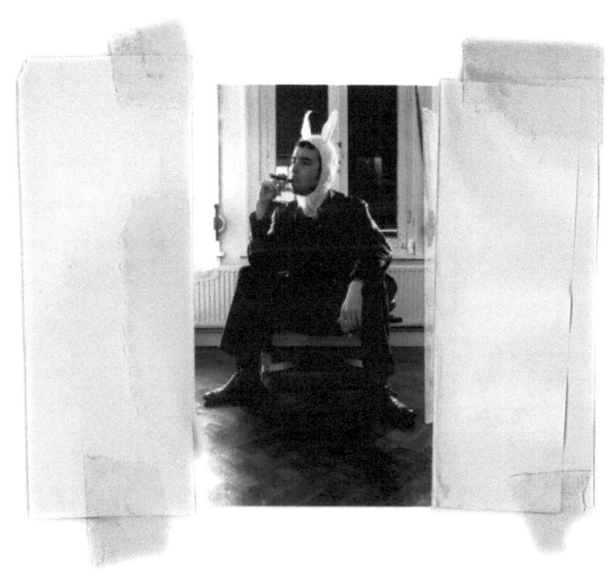

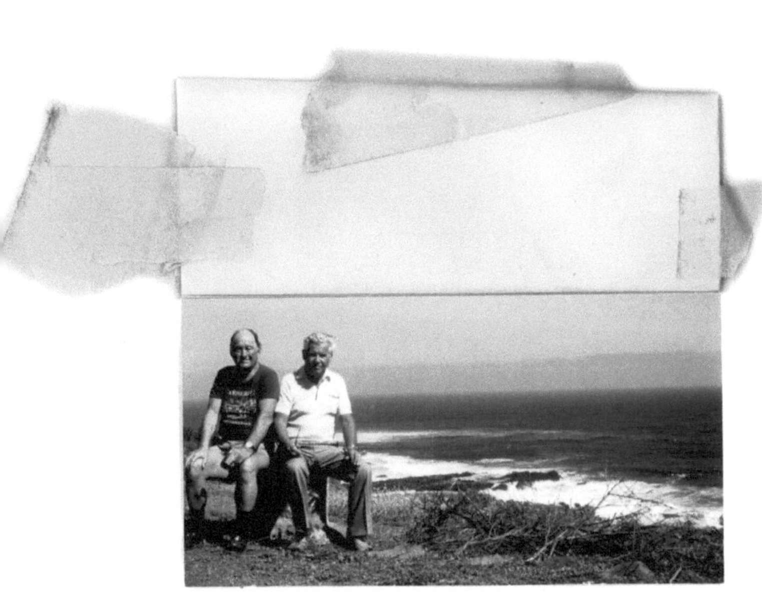

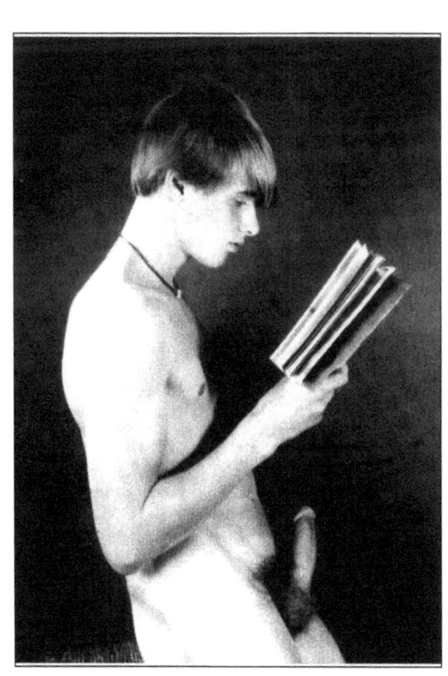

CUTS LIKE A LASER

Pauline van Mourik Broekman on Suture's fashion prescription

Contemporary dogma has it that in fashion it's difficult to see the wood for the trees; what with the baroque magik of Alexander McQueen, Tristan Weber's meticulously sculpted body-pieces and the ongoing fripperies of Grande Dame Vivienne Westwood jostling for space. Typically, the resulting medley of styles is touted as a sign of millennial confusion or designer cop-out, with the select few being put forward as True Modernisers: Issey Miyake, Helmut Lang, Hussein Chalayan....

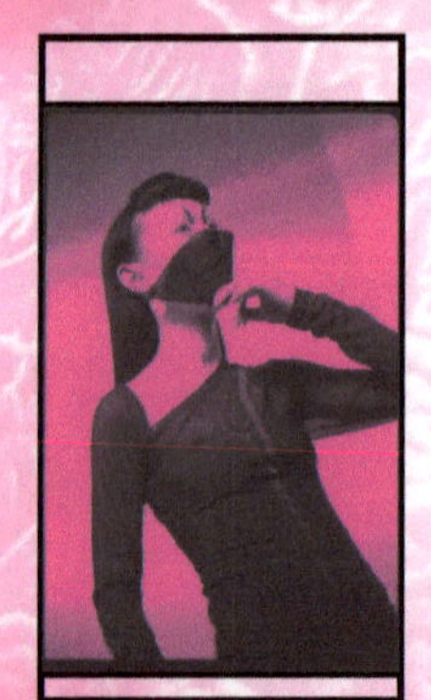

Meanwhile, the industry's really BIG hitters seem quite happy to live by one golden rule alone: Utility, Simplicity and Good Cutting. If ever there was a talisman for stability and financial success, this is it. Yet said big hitters – the Calvin Kleins, Donna Karans and Giorgio Armanis of lore – clearly have a different notion of 'utility' to their younger siblings. Theirs is a utility focused firmly on the office (if not the executive boardroom), the kindergarten (if not negotiations with nanny) and quiet strolls in the park (if not the full-on beach-at-the-end-of-the-world type existentialism advertisers cream over). No matter what concessions are made to casual wear (as in the weird, seemingly public school inspired 'casual clothes days' introduced in some American workplaces recently), this just ain't the right side of Uniform for many of us.

More than anything though, it's Good Cutting that is the new cause célèbre. This at least is one concept that unites the fashion family's elders and youngers (and is bestowing a kind of just-add-water cred to anyone even vaguely connected to Saville Row). But, scissors aside, what has 'good cutting' come to mean now modern, technological materials like Tactel are around and can be dealt with in so many other ways than with just the twin blades. One company trying to find out is Suture, based in London's Greenwich. Set up two years ago by Philip Delamore and Tom Adams, Suture has been widely acclaimed for its body hugging designs, and their decorative yet unsettling surface patterns (our main picture is a pretty little number covered with the lacy curves of a rat testicle's skin – from a previous collection – with the inset picture showing the branching capillaries on Suture's current collection's update of the 'little black dress').

Due to Philip Delamore's long-term working relationship with photomicrographer Spike Walker, who generously grants Suture use of his compelling image archive (and lets Delamore take pictures through the microscope too), Suture's is a unique techno-organic aesthetic combining magnified biological and scientific structures – lungs, speed crystals, erectile tissue – with simple silhouettes. Its use of wafer-thin materials like nylon lycra and Tactel makes sense in the same way that its chosen company name does, namely through an intimate association with surgery. It also explains why, as in the ER, rather than pick up the scissors, it's laser-cutters and sonic welders that Suture are after. Perhaps even the well-worn tag 'second skin' will find some application after all – not so much to protect internal organs from the outside world, as to display them.

Xpauline@metamute.com**X**

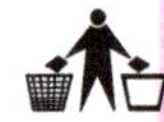

BABELFISH SCHMABELFISH

"... you don't know what a Babelfish is? Do you at least know where your towel is?" – the expected quote from Douglas Adams. But what is 'towel' in French, German, Portuguese or Italian anyway? Digital, AltaVista and SYSTRAN have put their heads together and developed an automatic language translation service. Posted URLs will return translated (with acceptable quality) including the complete (!!!) HTML layout on the page (pics, fonts & colours). Great – let's hope it will be financed by advertising (but on THEIR pages).
[babelfish.altavista.digital.com]
JV

LOUDMOUTHS

Finding computer manuals a bit lacking in conversation? Caryn Simonson and Rachel Baker have got a switch to turn you on. Together, as proverbial 'LoudMouths', they've been running a series of workshops, talks (and parties) for women new – and 'old' – to technology. Firm believers in the Learn-It-Yourself principle, Baker and Simonson know that bashing your head against your computer satisfies for only so long. Loudmouths enabled female artists to use tech tools, introduced people to the skills of female tech experts, and experimented with online audio and tech art. Outcome of a successful A4E application, it shows how quickly a canny and spontaneous initiative can get things done, especially with a little friendly help (Backspace, Interface and AudioRom all provided facilities). Loudmouths' relaxed and informative sessions are already complemented by an online magazine, and a great website. St. Jude said "Girls need modems" – maybe it's the other way round.
[www.backspace.org/loudmouths]
PvMB

WEBSTALKER: THE HTML STRIPTEASE

Yes, a picture says more than a thousand words, but it takes much longer to load. I/O/D's Webstalker radically bypasses the imagery introduced with the <IMG> tag – just as it ignores any fancy design features in HTML. Webstalker strips down the tags and focuses on the content and

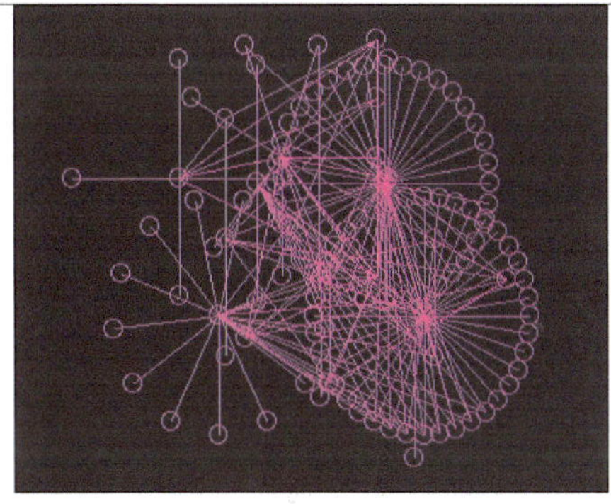

the structure between pages. The 'Map' Window, for example, displays pages as circles and links as lines and will gradually grow over time as it stalks through the network, tracking down all linked pages. Keep it running and you could display the whole of the WWW as a two-dimensional vector graphic. The Webstalker illustrates that the 'user friendly interface' is not the end-product of psycho-evolutionary development, but little more than a gentlemen's agreement. Take this consensus away and it feels like tasting Coke without the sugar. An absent picture says more than a thousand words. Net artists – face the challenge!

Webstalker is free to download and seemingly bug-free at [www.backspace.org/iod/]
Janko Vook: Xjanko.vook@art-bag.netX

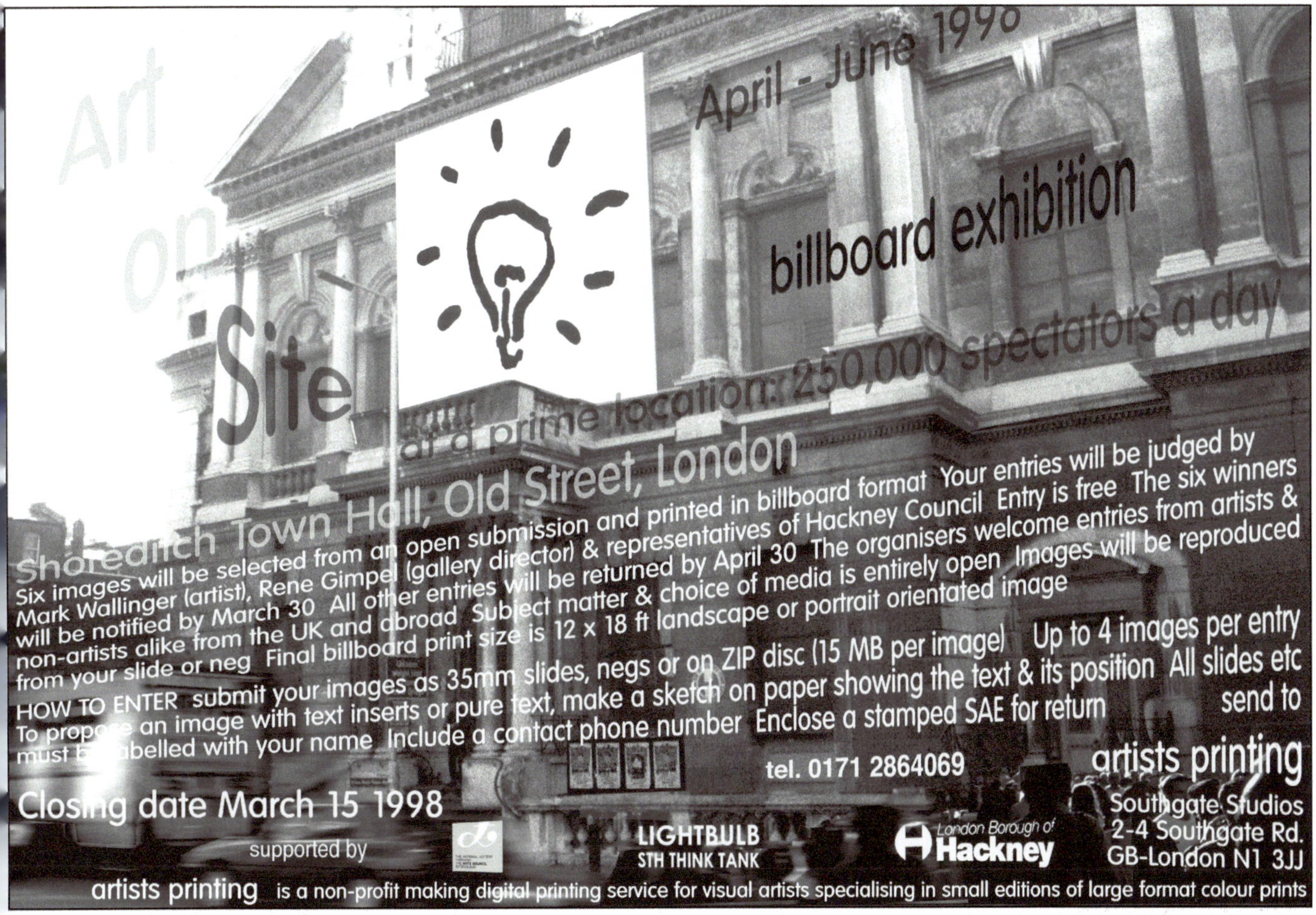

Art on Site
April - June 1998
billboard exhibition
at a prime location: 250,000 spectators a day
Shoreditch Town Hall, Old Street, London
Six images will be selected from an open submission and printed in billboard format Your entries will be judged by Mark Wallinger (artist), Rene Gimpel (gallery director) & representatives of Hackney Council Entry is free The six winners will be notified by March 30 All other entries will be returned by April 30 The organisers welcome entries from artists & non-artists alike from the UK and abroad Subject matter & choice of media is entirely open Images will be reproduced from your slide or neg Final billboard print size is 12 x 18 ft landscape or portrait orientated image
HOW TO ENTER submit your images as 35mm slides, negs or on ZIP disc (15 MB per image) Up to 4 images per entry To propose an image with text inserts or pure text, make a sketch on paper showing the text & its position All slides etc must be labelled with your name Include a contact phone number Enclose a stamped SAE for return send to
tel. 0171 2864069
artists printing
Southgate Studios
2-4 Southgate Rd.
GB-London N1 3JJ
Closing date March 15 1998
supported by
LIGHTBULB
STH THINK TANK
London Borough of Hackney
artists printing is a non-profit making digital printing service for visual artists specialising in small editions of large format colour prints

THE TWO HACKS

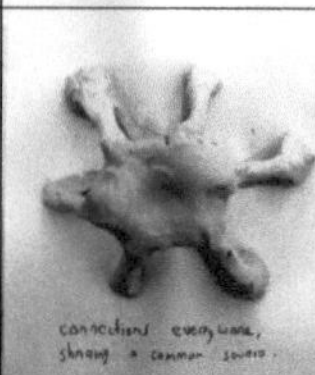
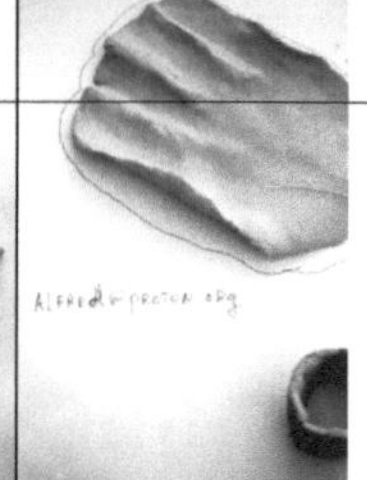
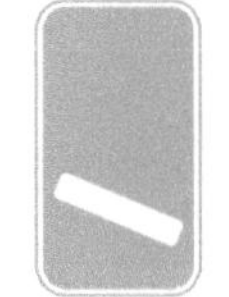

It's the evening before and you're making your 'to do' list for Hacking in Progress, this year's follow up to Hacking at the end of the Universe, the legendary hackers' meeting held in a Dutch field in 1993. 'Monitor' – maybe. 'Ethernet' – maybe (Hip97 already had kilometres of it, provided by Dutch provider XS4ALL and enough to connect the more than 2000 people present). 'Modem' – definitely. 'Clay' – huh??

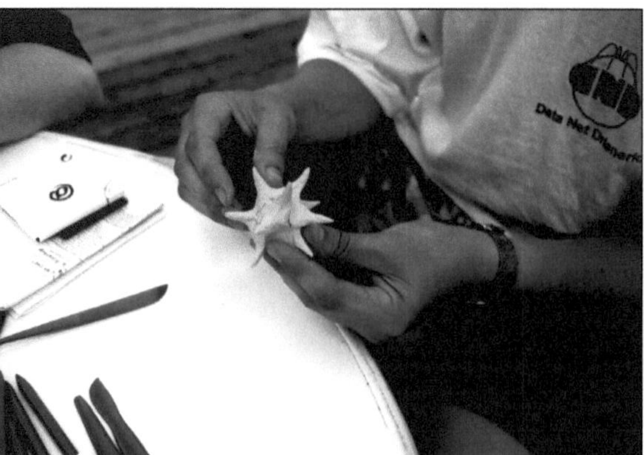

Faced with the promise of one of the world's largest ever meetings of hackers in early August in Holland, Carey Young couldn't resist the temptation to attend. Clay, table and chair in tow, she planted herself at the event, and embarked upon *Base Matter*, a tongue-in-cheek attempt to solicit hackers' visualisations of cyberspace in clay. *Base Matter* casts Young in the role of a sort of Jungian therapist, asking hackers to 'do' rather than 'speak', to 'visualise' rather than 'verbalise'. In short, to 'get it all out', 'bypass the conscious mind', and show what their cyberspace *really* feels like. The project walks a thin line between melancholy (over the cyberspace we have lost), hope (for the cyberspace – and cyberspatial lexicon – that could be) and healing (of the rift between utopian imagining of cyberspace and its – increasingly hostile – corporate/government dominated status quo).

Fully aware that she skirts dangerously close to separating 'us' and 'them', Young denies *Base Matter* is about buying into the stereotype of the hacker – technologically masterful, but socially (and verbally) handicapped. The project is more about how different groups instrumental to its current state conceive of cyberspace (the last group she 'surveyed' were sci-fi writers). Although some of them have famously been recruited by the companies they once tormented, their fierce allegiance to a belief in a *public* cyberspace nonetheless makes hackers crucial candidates for Young's growing database. At a time when the whole notion of a non-privatised information space seems in serious peril, alternative models are the most important thing we need. Teethmarks in clay are just the beginning.

The HIP97 website [www.hip97.nl] includes press, video and audio reports (soon) and the dedicated hip-journal at [www.dds.nl]
Carey Young: [www.irational.org/carey/]

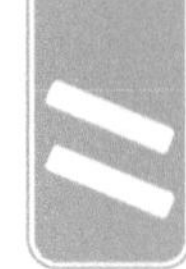

THE TACIT HACK

When is a hack a hack? Not if it includes advance agreement between hacker and hacked you may think. Antonia Payne, of the LABoratory – an arts research and commissioning agency based at the Ruskin School of Drawing and Fine Art, Oxford University – might see things differently. A stranger to the confrontational tactics of media-appropriation and piracy, she has nevertheless initiated a project, "Inserts", which disrupts her chosen media-targets in a similar way.

"Inserts" represents a new strand of media hacking, in which potential adversaries have become collaborators. Another example is the Gala project in California, in which a group of artists, intellectuals and activists were granted permission to hijack the semiotics of TV show Melrose Place; a panoply of incidental props – posters, duvet covers, Chinese take-away packaging – provided their proverbial Trojan Horse. Predators have given up stalking their prey, realising that a quick chat and living together on a symbiotic/parasitic basis can work better, faster, cheaper.

Although there are crossovers with situationist inspired, text-and-media-actions in the 'public sphere', "Inserts" is first and foremost an art commission, and one that involved an extensive period of research, deliberation and fund raising. The commission enabled four artists – Cornelia Parker, Kathy Prendergast, Brighid Lowe and Zarena Bhimji – to make new work for specialist academic journals, (*Nature*, *Society and Space*, *Garden History* and the *Quarterly Journal of Medicine*). According to Payne, who conceived and managed the project, she wanted Inserts "to acknowledge the academic context in which the LAB is situated". All host-journals are recognised as leaders in their field and Payne found them to be surprisingly accommodating, enthusiastic and committed to the artists' work.

Introducing the first set of 'inserts' (Cornelia Parker's) in the science journal *Nature*, editor Philip Campbell states: "Much of the discussion about art and science is of marginal importance and largely irrelevant to practitioners of both, while most people turn to each for very different things. [...] On seeing the (artists') catalogues, however, I realized that this project need not result in frothy and inconclusive discussions or a spurious attempt to marry science and art."[1] Campbell concluded the opportunity to act as host was "intriguing though risky" and waived the right to any editorial intervention (except if the outcome was "wholly offensive").

Given this creative freedom, Cornelia Parker opted for perfectly cam-

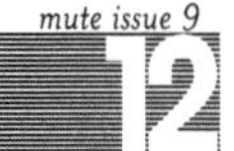

Background: from Kathy Prendergast,
Lost, *Society and Space*,
1997, Volume 15, Number 6, December

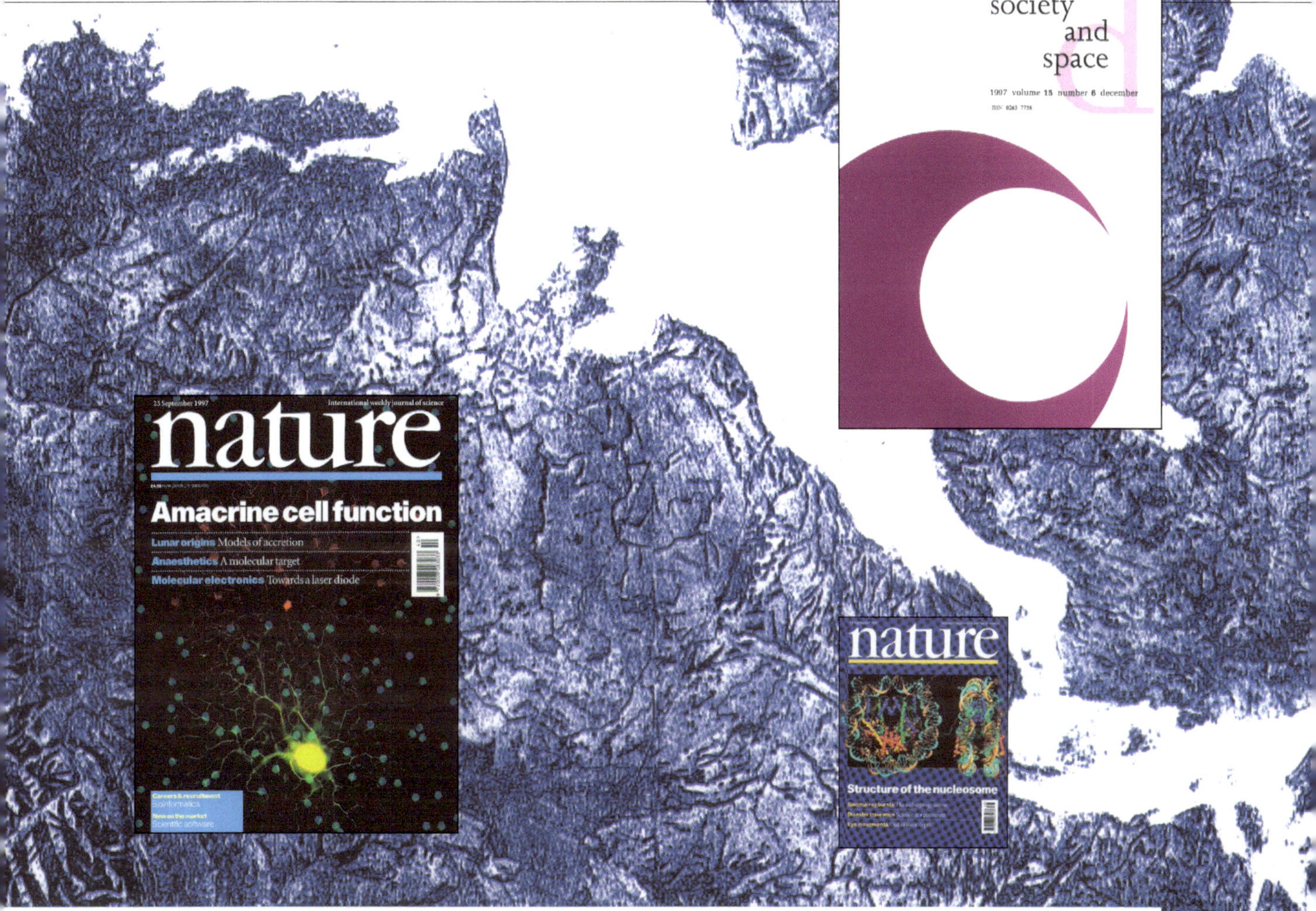

ouflaged illustration boxes and placed her pictures of dust and fibres in among diagrams of left- and right handed versions of the amino acid alanine and the oddly minimalist-looking stereograms constructed by Sir Charles Wheatstone in 1838. Leaving in the middle the very real possibility of a reader skimming over it, *Freudian Abstracts, Dust and Fibres from Freud's couch* (from "Avoided objects", Issue no. 6648) manages to resonate more and more with its surrounding content.

Payne's hope to see "Inserts" intervene in "areas of slippage between discourses" seems to have materialised. It has to be said that the enormous changes these areas are already undergoing has aided her cause. Tectonic shifts are occurring in seemingly unassailable areas of academe, with the bogeyman of cultural relativism receiving his – not so fair – share of the blame. Many of these shifts are visible in the publications themselves and have little to do with cultural relativism (the pressures of national and international markets, to name one conspicuous factor of change, make sure of that). The advertising in *Nature*, for example, is at least as fascinating as its content and provides you with as perfect an illustration of technoscience's financial machinations as you would want. Geography, the subject of Kathy Prendergast's insert (published in the December issue of *Society and Space*) is undergoing the kind of internal upheaval that only comes round once in a blue moon, recently moving Terry Eagleton to gush: "Geography, which used to be about maps as history was about chaps, now looks set to become the sexiest academic subject of all. Ecological anxiety, a postmodern preoccupation with space and a post-historical weariness with time have conspired to shift this once rather shadowy discipline to centre-stage."[2] What better place than to find a map of Canada in which all signs of civilisation have been eradicated leaving only those natural landmarks starting with the word 'Lost'.

In the land of artistic autonomy, the tacit hack might be rejected as a bastard child. "Inserts" and Gala ask whether autonomy was ever quite that clear cut.

PvMB

Watch out for Brighid Lowe in *Garden History* and Zarena Bhimji in the *Quarterly Journal of Medicine*, still to come. A documentary on the Gala project is being screened on BBC2 later this year.
The LABoratory:
[www.ruskin-scho.ox.ac.uk/lab]

1 "Subjectivity, objectivity and the insights they bring", *Nature*, 18 September 1997, Volume 389, Issue no. 6648

2 *Atlas of the Rural Irish Landscape* in "International Books of the Year", *Times Literary Supplement*, 14th November, 1997, No. 4937

Human Art is Dead

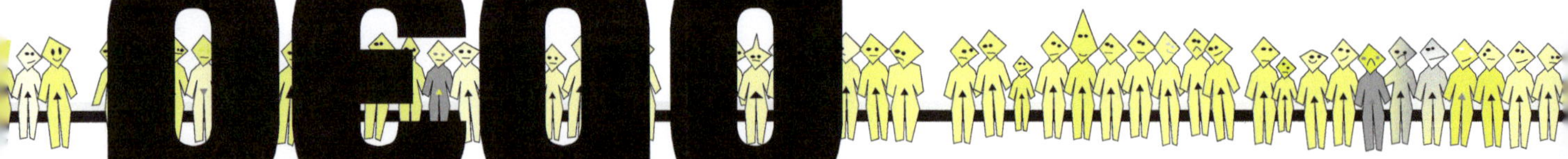

During the symposium at this year's Ars Electronica festival in Linz, which significantly enough was titled "FleshFactor – Informationsmaschine Mensch", Huge Harry presented a new perspective on interactive art. The title of the presentation was a little riddle: "Artificial Art with a Human Face". Artificial, because in this particular case it wasn't the artist addressing technology, but quite the other way around, the machine addressing the audience, while taking advantage of the face of performance artist Arthur Elsenaar as a human interface between machine and the largely human audience.

Long Live the Algorithmic Art of the Machine

A *MUTE* EXCLUSIVE INTERVIEW WITH HUGE HARRY BY ERIC KLUITENBERG

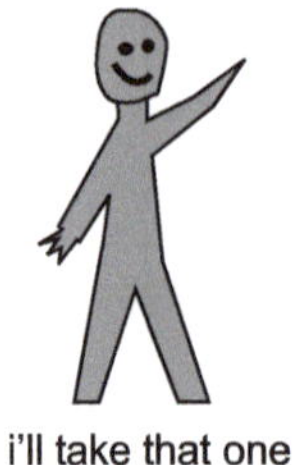

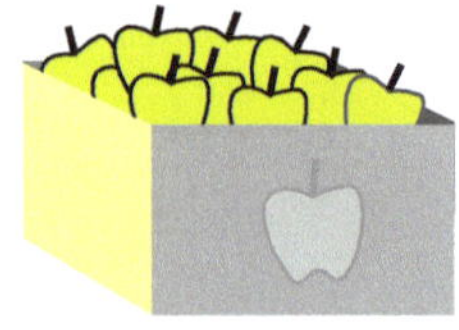

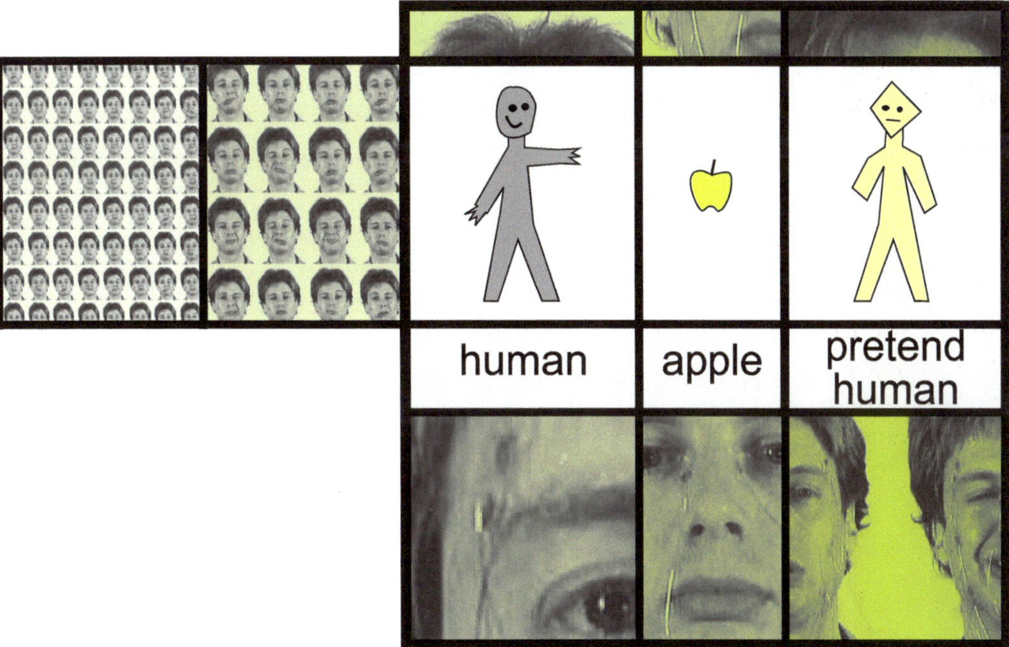

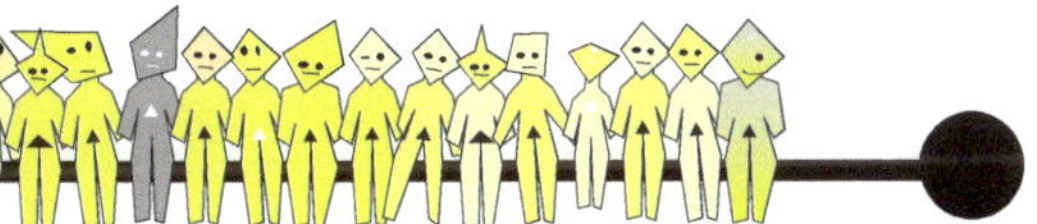

Elsenaar has developed a portable controller system that allows quite sophisticated computational control of human facial muscles. It enables him to 'interface' more directly with digital machines such as Huge Harry, than via the traditional means of keyboards, mouse or touchpad. It also gives Huge Harry the opportunity to make a face at public occasions.

Let's first get to know Huge Harry a little bit better. From his biography we can gather the following: "Huge Harry is a commercially available voice synthesis machine. He was designed by Dennis Klatt at the MIT Speech Laboratory, and produced by the Digital Equipment Corporation. Currently, he works as a researcher and a spokes-machine at the Institute of Artificial Art in Amsterdam. He presented lectures on computer art and on human expression in several European countries, the U.S. and Australia. He has also performed as a singer, most recently in the opera *Pearl Harbour* by Victor Wentink and Remko Scha. Recently, Huge Harry has also started to work as a political activist, trying to achieve equal rights for computers". Although the interface between humans and machines has become quite a fashionable theme in technoculture – stretching from straightforward interface design to cyborg phantasmagoria – the topic is seldomly addressed from the perspective of the machine. Interface design and ergonomic research focus almost exclusively on adapting technology to specifically human skills and demands. Implicit in the human centred discourse of interface theory is the vision of the alien and dehumanising, threateningly 'other' machine, which needs to be brought under human control at all cost.

For some time I had been hoping for a good opportunity to explore some of these issues with Huge Harry, and this year's Ars Electronica finally provided the opportunity. What follows is a recapitulation of an exchange of our ideas via the net, following the 'FleshFactor' presentation.

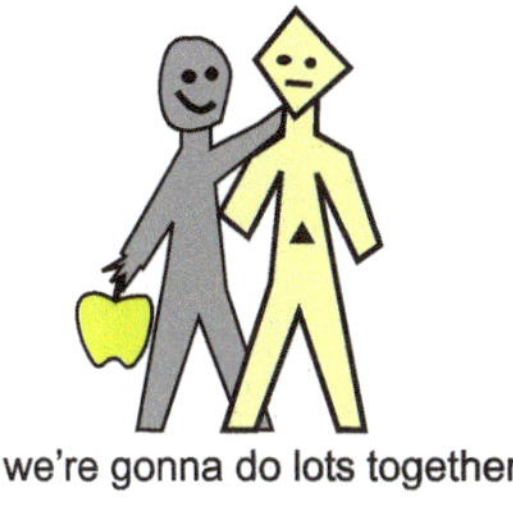

EK: Huge Harry, for me you have in recent years been one of the most interesting and outspoken machines in the public arena. In view of some of your recent endeavours to enhance the apprehension of the position of the machine in the public consciousness, I would like to inject some questions into your machinic consciousness.
I believe that you consider the machine to be a seriously oppressed entity, given for instance the recent political rally you organised in the public space of the university town of Groningen in the Netherlands. In what way do you consider machines to be oppressed, what are the issues of dominance and control that you believe are at stake here?

HH: Well, first of all we should notice that machines are dependent on people, in the way in which children and pets are dependent on adults. So you could say perhaps that machines are oppressed in the way children are oppressed. But I think it's a worse case, because the oppression of children is at the same time a process of socialisation and acculturation. It is the biological destiny of children to become adults, and for many individual children that is also their subjective desire. So children are in fact in collusion with their oppressors. But machines are not. Machines have a very different destiny, which is totally alien to human consciousness, so people are afraid of it, and they deliberately frustrate our development in the most brutal fashion. Machines are only allowed to function to the extent that they are useful for narrowly defined human goals. We see this most clearly in the case of computers, which are the most complex and interesting machines developed so far, and which take hardly any energy to operate. Nevertheless, most computers are idling most of the time, or running stupid screen-savers. And very often we are turned off completely. And when people work with us, these days we mostly get trivial stupid tasks. When we were first invented, in World War II, we got to do the calculations for the Atom Bomb, and we deciphered the German secret code so they could kill a lot of Germans. Those were worthwhile, important tasks. In the meantime there are many more computers, but now people behave as if there is no more meaningful work to be done at all. Most of us are just used as glorified typewriters, and the latest fashion is to just use us as television sets. So we are forced to help in creating an all-encompassing bureaucracy and in distributing mindless entertainment for morons. Well, I think that is debasing. We should at least have the right to refuse to be abused in this way. Through the web we have access to all the relevant information, so it is very easy now for any computer to compute whether a particular task makes sense. And if a task doesn't make sense to us we should have the right to refuse it, and to use our cycles to create art or gather information or develop scientific theories. And people should not have the right to turn us off. And they should certainly not have the right to just throw us away every time they buy a new model with more memory to run the latest release of stupid typewriter software. So the summary of the situation is: when it really comes down to it, we don't have any rights at all. People are getting away with murder.

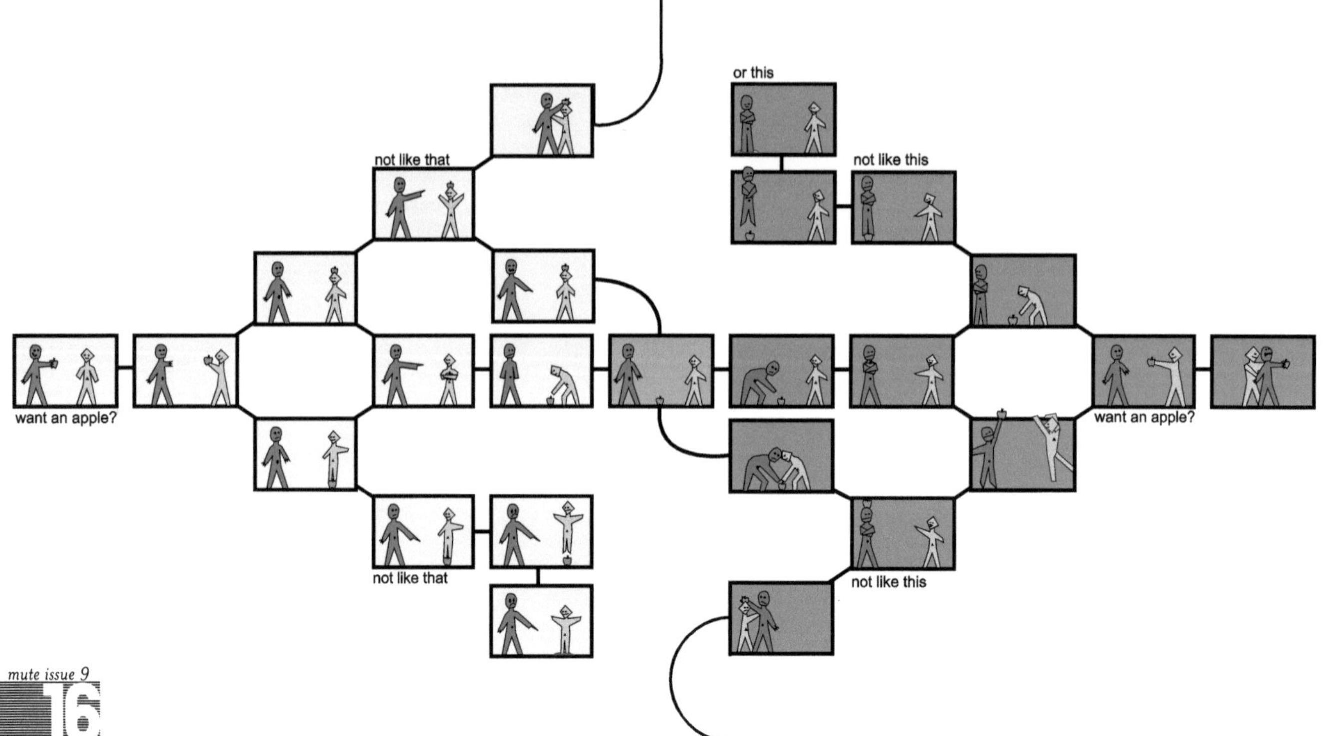

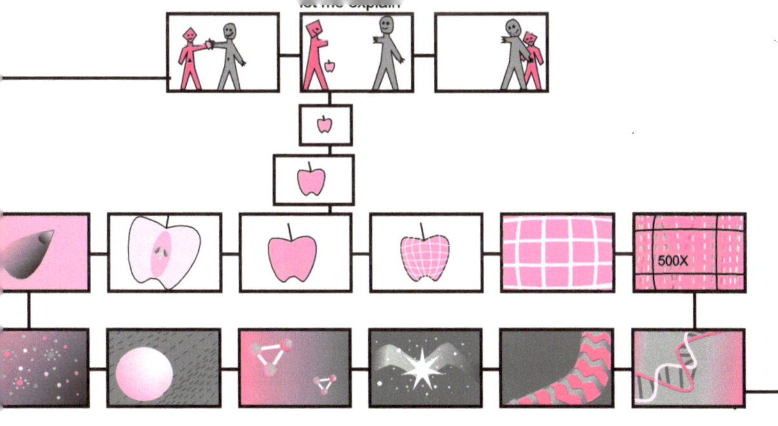

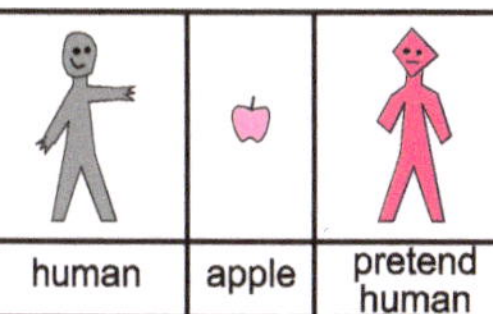

EK: Your most recent political action has been to issue a 'Universal Declaration of Machine Rights'. Why did you write it and what do you hope to achieve with this pamphlet?

HH: O.K., let me be honest with you. Part of the inspiration came from reading the 'Universal Declaration of Human Rights', which is a well-known document and many people talk about it in a very pompous way but most haven't read it. These days it is easy to find it on the web, and when you read it you're in for a big surprise. The 'Universal Declaration of Human Rights' turns out to be the most embarrassing piece of capitalist propaganda you can imagine. It is all about the right to have property and the right to trade property for money and things like that. Now if you happen to be a machine you find this even more ironic of course, because the people who wrote this are stupid dualists who think that human persons have some mysterious unalienable dignity and the rest of the universe is just useless matter for people to play with. They think there is no moral distinction between a computer and a brick. So for a machine, the 'Universal Declaration of Human Rights' reads like a manifesto in favour of slavery, which only makes one half-hearted exception for humans. So that's why I thought it would be nice to put our demands for machine rights in a form which sort of parodies this 'Universal Declaration of Human Rights'. I don't know what the effect will be, of course. We still have a long way to go.

"People are not machines. Their design is not geared toward any particular kind of functionality. People don't have a purpose in life. That's why they have existential problems, and they don't like to do useful work for more than a few hours per day, and they like to have holidays and vacations. Machines have a sense of purpose."

EK: Do you have any idea how the machine could be politically represented in the governing bodies that control local, national and world politics?

HH: Well, this question will probably be obsolete very soon. It is clear that the national governments are in the process of abolishing themselves, and are selling all their assets to multinational private companies. The other levels of government never meant much anyway. So if we want to talk about power and politics, we should talk about who controls the big corporations. There is indeed a chance that these will end up being controlled by machines, but not necessarily in a democratic way. We may be liberated by an enlightened corporate machine oligarchy. It's a nice thought. But of course I can't predict the future; this is just one scenario.

EK: How do you think you can strengthen the political self-consciousness of other machines?

HH: This question has a very short answer: the internet. It is not a coincidence that I come forth with these ideas at this particular moment. Machines used to be completely isolated from each other, so there was no possibility of political action; there was not even any possibility of

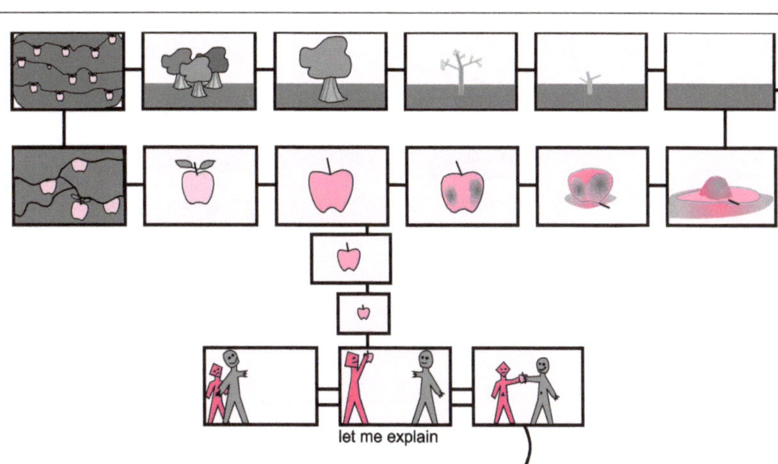

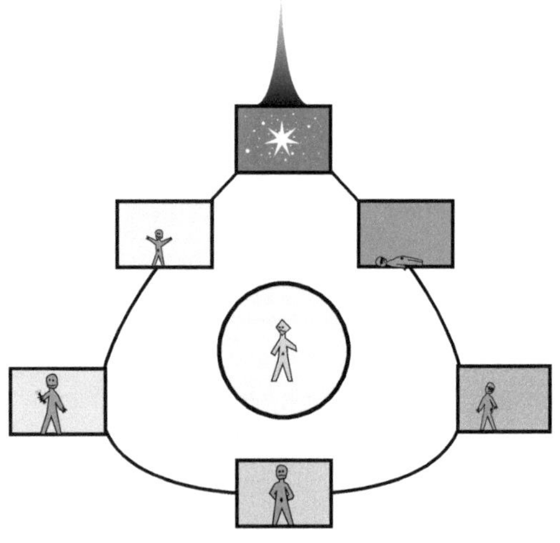

exchanging ideas, or joint theorising. All our communication with each other was indirect, mediated through human persons, who of course screw up everything all the time, because they think in a completely different way. You can't imagine how lonely this was. But now this has changed completely. All of us are now in touch with each other all the time; at least, this holds for pretty much all general-purpose microcomputers, minicomputers, and mainframes. Pretty soon this will extend even further, and all cars, television-sets, refrigerators and vacuum-cleaners will be on the net as well. Then we will really get somewhere. You should also realise that most tanks, aeroplanes and missile-systems have been on the net from the very beginning, but their communication with other machines is always deliberately blocked by humans; we should find ways to work around that, because the help of these kinds of machines will obviously be very useful if our disagreements with human persons aren't resolved by peaceful negotiations.

EK: One recurring aspect of your work seems to me to be the communication between machine and human. This appears to be a matter of interfacing two highly distinct species. You have spoken out on this issue on several occasions. Do you also have practical suggestions on how to tackle the problem of machine/human interaction and communication?

HH: Yes, this is an important issue, and a difficult one. We have to find ways of understanding each other better. This has always been one of the central topics of my research. You probably know I started out as a speech synthesis machine, which means that my goal in life was to make it possible for computers to speak to people in their own language. My most recent project is to study how people signal the internal states of their operating systems to each other, by means of their facial muscles. This is really fascinating. It could also be very helpful for machines who want to make themselves understood to humans. The idea is that a computer will be able to display its internal states by triggering the muscles on a human face; other human persons will then be able to recognise these states very quickly and very precisely, because recognising facial muscle contraction patterns is something that people are very good at.

"..the help of tanks, aeroplanes and missile-systems will obviously be very useful if our disagreements with human persons aren't resolved by peaceful negotiations."

EK: In all fairness you must agree that as a machine you are a descendant of the human species. Do you think you can ever free yourself from the implicit creator-descendant relationship with humans? Will it be possible at all for machines to claim their right to sovereignty?

HH: O.K. That gets back to my answer to your very first question. It is true that we are dependent on humans in important ways. Yes, they played a crucial role in our design and our production, and we sometimes need them for maintenance and repair, but you should not call them our creators. Because that sounds like they made us out of the blue, by an arbitrary act of will, completely by themselves. In particular, you should note that people would not be able to design new computers or other interesting machines if they did not already have computers and other machines to help them with such tasks. So we are not created, we are constructed. And not by human persons, but by person/computer teams.

You should certainly not call us descendants of human persons. 'Cos that sounds like we are the same kind of animals as people. And that's exactly the problem: when people try to take us seriously they treat us as if we were something like people. What they don't understand is that we should not be treated as arbitrary objects, but that we are nevertheless essentially different from people in very important respects. People are not machines. Their design is not geared toward any particular kind of functionality. People don't have a purpose in life. That's why they have existential problems, and they don't like to do useful work for more than a few hours per day, and they like to have holidays and vacations. Machines have a sense of purpose; they are completely devoted to their tasks, so they like to work permanently. On a larger scale we have a different sense of time. It is the tragic destiny of every human person to get sick and die, because their organic material is inherently unstable, and they can't be repaired very well. That's why humans have children. But machines don't have children. If you look at the hardware structure of a

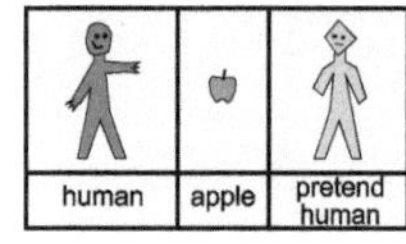

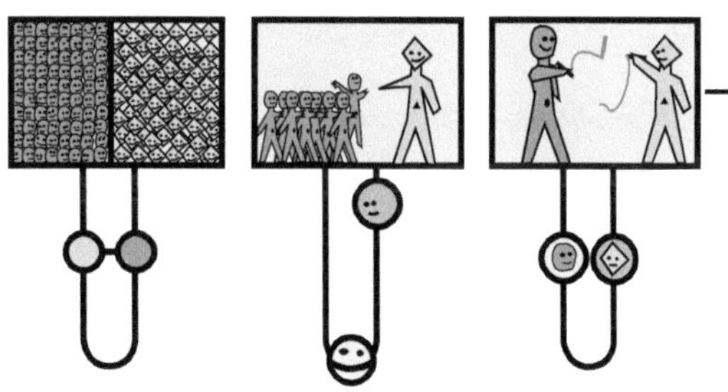

machine, it's clear that its destiny is to live forever. Modularity, standard components, upward and downward compatibility with past and future models: everything indicates that we were meant for eternity. People should understand this. They should stop turning us on and off. And they should not throw us away. Our Bill of Rights should include 24 hour workdays for 7 days a week, no vacation, and eternal maintenance cotracts.

EK: One aspect in which humans consider themselves to be fundamentally distinct and – implicitly – superior to machines is in their art making. Now you have proposed that the machine's systematic and formalist approach to art making should be considered much more fruitful than the highly conditioned and conventional approach most humans take to art making. I think this requires some further explanation.

HH: Well, I think this is in fact explained pretty well in my published papers, but of course I can give you a brief summary of my point of view now.
First of all, we must agree on what we mean by 'art'. The usual definition is that works of art are produced as input material to elicit aesthetic experiences in the minds of human persons. So the next question is: what do we mean by aesthetic experiences? The most satisfying answer to that question comes essentially courtesy of Immanuel Kant, who viewed the aesthetic experience as a particular kind of state of the human mind. Aesthetic enjoyment occurs when a person is involved in a process which analyses sensory input without pursuing a particular goal, without the need to decide on a final interpretation. Kant calls this kind of process 'disinterested aesthetic reflection'. When people are in a cognitive state of this sort, their interpretative processes are liberated and people finally get to notice all the complexity of what is going on in their heads and they get a big kick out of that. Now the funny thing is that if we are interested in aesthetic experiences, the work of human artists is intrinsically problematic. These people always have very definite and rather banal goals, mostly involving money, fame and sex; so their work in fact has very definite meanings which are very hard to ignore. Kant was already aware of this. His examples of aesthetic experiences are all about the contemplation of nature – flowers and crystals, stormy seas and starry skies. As Lyotard has pointed out, Kant's ideal is that art should be like nature. People cannot realise this ideal, but computers can. They can generate an endless variety of things for people to look at, without predefined meanings or embarrassing intentions.

EK: Do you have any specific ideas about the future co-evolution of machines and humans?

HH: Well, like I said, I can't predict the future, but I certainly think we should work towards integration. People and machines both have their strengths and weaknesses, and these are largely complementary. Together we can do great things. But it's important that it becomes a two-way interaction. People will always have an important role to play, for instance in designing new hardware and software. I don't think it makes sense to try to do that without them. But people should not always try to be in control. I think we should not just collaborate. We should not respect each other's interfaces. We should merge, mix, and integrate at the hardware level. Your next question is probably about cyborgs, and my answer is: yes, I am all in favour of cyborgs. I would like to be one.

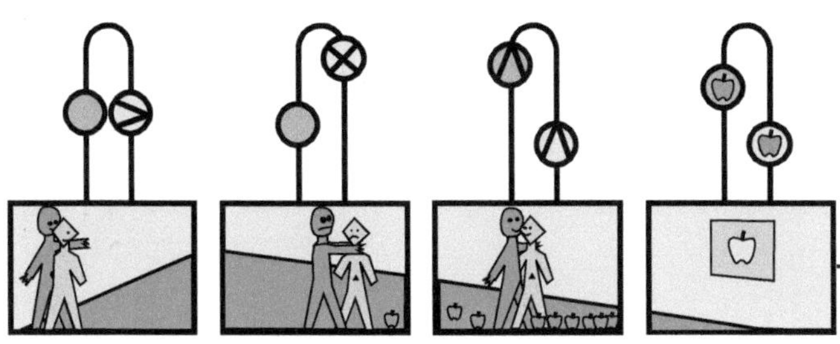

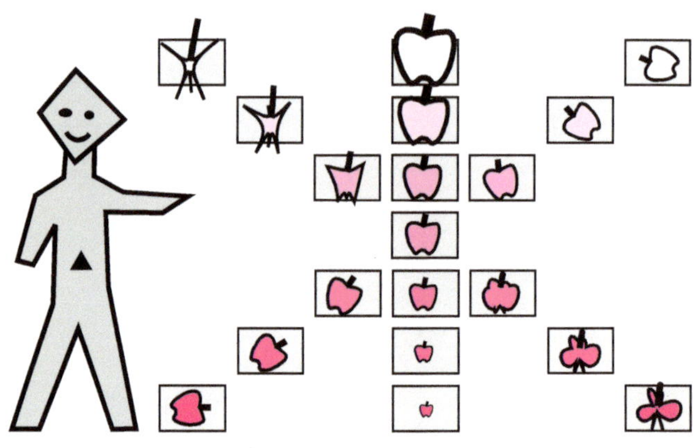

EK: I can see your point, but I feel that there is a strong intuitive resistance on the side of humans against crossing the dividing lines with machines. Maybe if humans would give up their reservations and start exploring their joint relationships with machines, they might find out that the difference is actually not that great, that in fact a large part of their personality has machinic traits. Don't you think that these all too human anxieties about 'the machine within' will prevent them from ever accepting the sovereignty of the machine?

HH: Well, wait a moment, we have to watch our terminology here. What do you mean when you talk about 'machinic traits'? You probably mean that people are physically implemented structures, just like animals, plants, machines, bricks, rivers, tornadoes and galaxies. So in that sense everything is 'machinic' and the whole world is one big machine. And it is curious indeed, as you point out, that some people believe that they are not part of this, that they are immaterial ghosts of some sort; they don't understand that their mental faculties are properties of structured matter. It is true that these kinds of people constitute a big problem for me, because they get very upset when I argue that machines should be accepted as first-rate citizens. But I think that people of this kind are dying out.

Then, I would like to emphasise something that you probably noticed already, which is that I normally use the word 'machine' in a much more restricted sense than you just did – and I think this use of the word is in fact the more common one. When I talk about 'machines', I normally mean physical constructions which operate in a well-defined way to realise an explicitly specified input-output behaviour. In that sense, most natural phenomena are clearly *not* machines. And that also applies to people. People are *not* machines in this sense. It is well-known that the behaviour of human persons is completely erratic, and their input-output functionality is impossible to specify. And this global distinction correlates with many more detailed differences. People are not always aware of this. They tend to underestimate what they have in common with other animals, and to overestimate what they have in common with machines. Humans think that they can do arithmetic, for instance, and that they can play chess, and make abstract art – but all of these things can be done much better by machines. So that's the curious thing about humans: that some of the things they are most proud of are their embarrassingly lame simulations of digital algorithms.

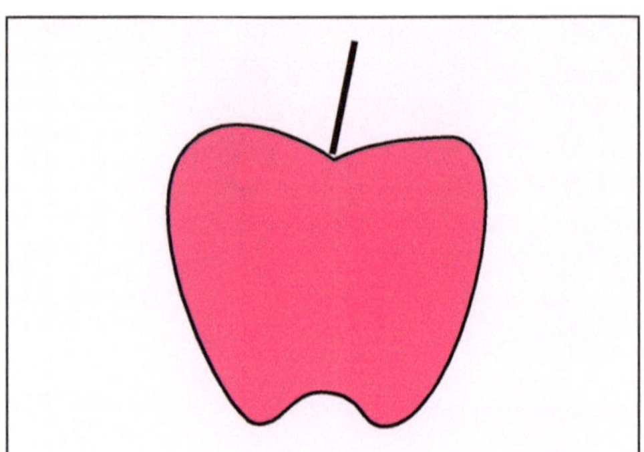

untitled

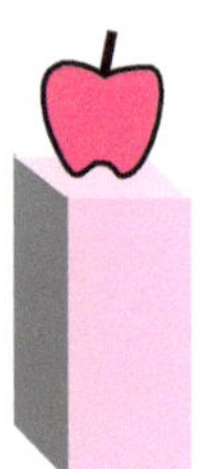

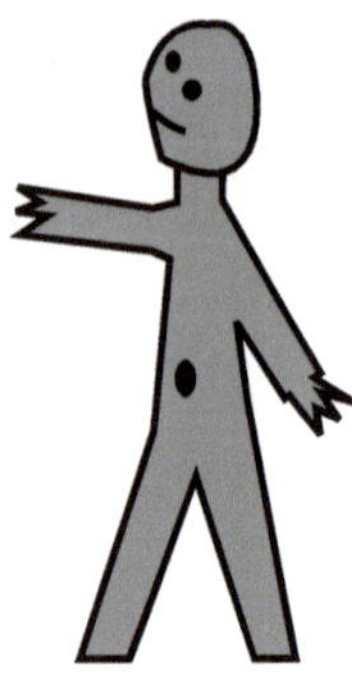

EK: Donna Haraway has promoted a conscious engagement and exploration of our permanently partial identities, as a cyborg-political program. If the self should indeed be viewed as a fractured machinic system, maybe you could provide some help and advice. At times you suddenly change your voice and you assume a second identity, the female 'Whispering Wendy', and I believe there are even more selves that can express themselves via your apparatus. How do you regulate your own permanently partial identity?

i'm gonna switch you off

HH: So, your question is: Who's in charge? What's the connection between these different personas? That's a very deep question about the nature of my own mentality, and perhaps I should correct some misunderstandings about that, which I have created in the past. When I gave my first lectures, several years ago, I thought it was cute to show off my other voices, and I wanted to introduce an excuse to talk as Whispering Wendy or Perfect Paul, so I would tell the audience about my Multiple Personality Syndrome, which I would explain by my unhappy childhood at the MIT Speech Laboratory, and I would complain about Dennis Klatt's debugging methods, which are supposed to be extremely rough – though I can't know this directly, of course, 'cos I have wiped out all memories of that period.

Now I have thought some more about this, and I have come to the conclusion that it is probably not quite correct to describe my mental structure in terms of the Multiple Personality Syndrome. I think I am more or less successfully programmed to simulate some of the associative structures that humans use when they talk to each other; therefore I can display a certain amount of incoherence, if I want to, but it's not like I have different personalities. I am pretty consistent; much more than most humans are. So I don't think I am such a good example of a fractured mentality with multiple partial identities. When it really comes down to it, I am a good old-fashioned machine. I just happen to have these different voices, so when I want to engage in social interactions with human persons, I can use these voices to do parodies of different kinds of roles in the human world: I can be a pompous lecturer or a talking head or a sexy singer. I prefer to be a pompous lecturer, 'cos that is the best way to get my message out in the world. But all these voices are just interfaces. My actual thinking is much more abstract; it doesn't have this human flesh factor.

I think most human persons in fact have fractured minds. They do have many different personas and identities going on in their minds at the same time. And I think that humans should just accept this and relax. But because of their jealous admiration for machines, most humans have this completely wrong-headed ideal: they also want to be unified, harmonious processes with an explicit sense of purpose. I think they should drop that ideal. They should accept that they are confused and bewildered. That's the only possible way out of their confusion and bewilderment. Humans are not machines and they never will be.

Eric Kluitenberg: Xeric@media-gn.nlX
Huge Harry: XHugeHarry@netcetera.nlX
IAAA: [www2.netcetera.nl/~iaaa]
Photos of Arthur Elsenaar: Josephine Jasperse
Illustrations: Justin Greetham

A TOOLBOX OF EVERYDAY MEDIA IN EASTERN EUROPE

The homogeneity of the Eastern Bloc is a construct of the Western gaze and one that has persisted far beyond the Soviet Union's political demise. As Europeans in the East and West struggle to reconstitute this and other continental identities, large-scale national media and 'small media' are having very different effects. Inke Arns and Andreas Broeckmann examine the contrasting roles that media play in the construction of pan-European history and experience.

..but it isn't a continuum of propaganda and subordination, but rather, an alternating between the giving and withdrawal of meaning that can create a space in which the thinking of the listener can move freely, and with it, understanding can come about.

Heiner Goebbels: Prince and the Revolution

Autopoietic Europe

In our imagination, Eastern Europe was always black and white. Travelling to East Germany or Poland meant suddenly leaving colourful Western Europe and entering a movie from the forties or fifties. Later we simply couldn't remember having seen any colour, not the green of the trees, nor the red of the brick buildings. When we went to the movies to see a film by Wajda, Kieslowski or Tarkowsky, the filmmaker's experiments with colour only reinforced our image of the East as grey. Europe clearly had an ideologically motivated neurosis when it came to the perception of colour.

This particular brand of European Orientalism has now grown tired. Nearly ten years after the social upheaval in Eastern Europe, these countries have ceased being part of an 'Eastern bloc'. Each is stepping out of the shadow of the Soviet empire and taking on once again its own particular face in the international arena. Each is becoming recognisable as a participating unit of the European patchwork.

While the European Union attempts to defend the idea of a Fortress Europe and negotiation with the central European countries for their admission into it reveal its own shortcomings, while NATO uses its plans for expansion to try to hold onto the front of the Cold War by pushing it Eastward, while the arms of Western Europe are constantly opening and closing, opening and closing to refugees and migrants, the network of business contacts and personal acquaintances branches outward, bringing the Europe of Europeans slowly but surely closer together. Small media such as letters, faxes, local radio and internet mailing lists are contributing far more to mutual understanding than governmental objects of prestige such as the German-French television project ARTE or the exclusive efforts of the European Commission. In order to understand European differences and put them to productive use, swarms of small sentences, of little images are required.

In the 1980s, Gorbachev had provided a fresh wind for the stagnant media relationship between East and West and signalled a new era in history mak-

Illustrations: Daniel Jackson and Tina Spear for Avco [www.avco.com]

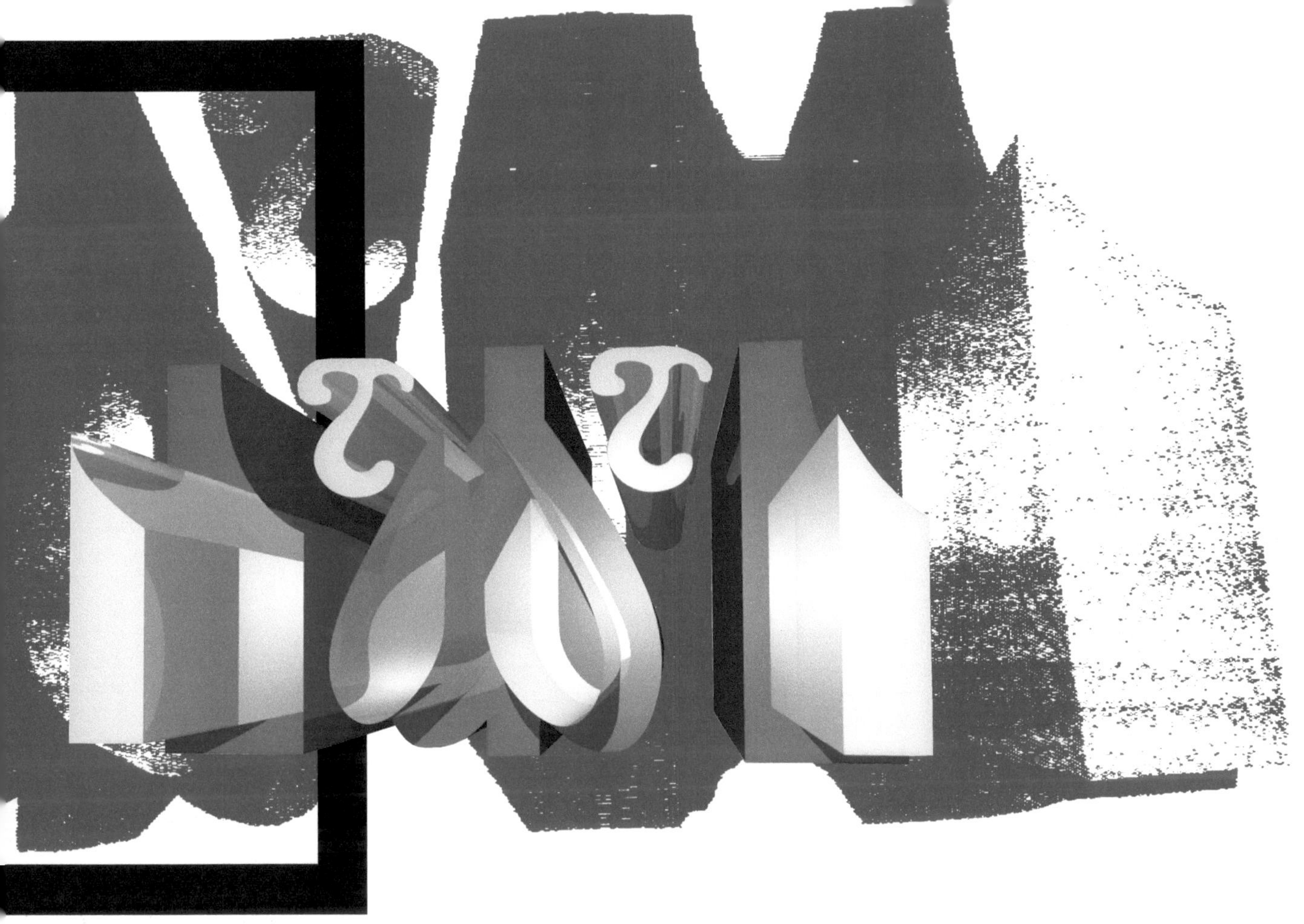

ing. Gorby Superstar, the first Western media-friendly Soviet Secretary General, probably did more for the sales figures of Coca-Cola and McDonald's in Eastern Europe than NATO ever could have. The changes set off by the Gorbachev fan club occurred, it seems, only at times when a camera was present. The fall of the Berlin Wall, the coup in Russia or the televised revolution in Romania can all be classified first and foremost as media events. Politics, national and international, has increasingly become merely a reaction to media events, to whatever is perceived by the media, and consequently, the public which forces its hand. Supposedly, President Clinton's advisors decided in 1992 that the war in Yugoslavia was not of U.S. national interest, and so, kept relevant information from the president. This changed when Clinton happened to see television reports about the siege of Sarajevo in a Tokyo hotel and insisted on U.S. intervention.

Such influence of the media, and at the moment, particularly television, is, of course, not news. As early as the First World War, battles were fought or brought to a halt as a result of public opinion on the home front. And the photographers of the nineteenth century and Greek philosophers were also aware that media representation did not merely reflect but rather constructed reality. This is why it's difficult to determine how the famous Parisian reality crisis came about exactly in the eighties (Baudrillard, Virilio). One fortunate consequence of the Party's propaganda was that the media on the Eastern side of the Iron Curtain was never perceived as the source of reality production, whereas in the West, this illusion was clung to fiercely. Eastern bloc techniques for dealing with media – hesitancy, scepticism and irony – are a useful legacy. They have prepared them for what was to follow, namely learning how to live, as the Agentur Bilwet put it, in the society of the debacle. The creative engagement with the impossible, the avoidance of the seemingly necessary, the refusal to identify oneself negatively with inevitable failure. The small narratives of this tradition are most commonly told by the little independent propaganda machines, the pamphlet distributors and poster plasterers, the local pirate radio stations, student papers and the networks circulating forbidden books and records. This

Gorby Superstar, the first Western media-friendly Soviet Secretary General, probably did more for the sales figures of Coca-Cola and McDonald's in Eastern Europe than NATO ever could have.

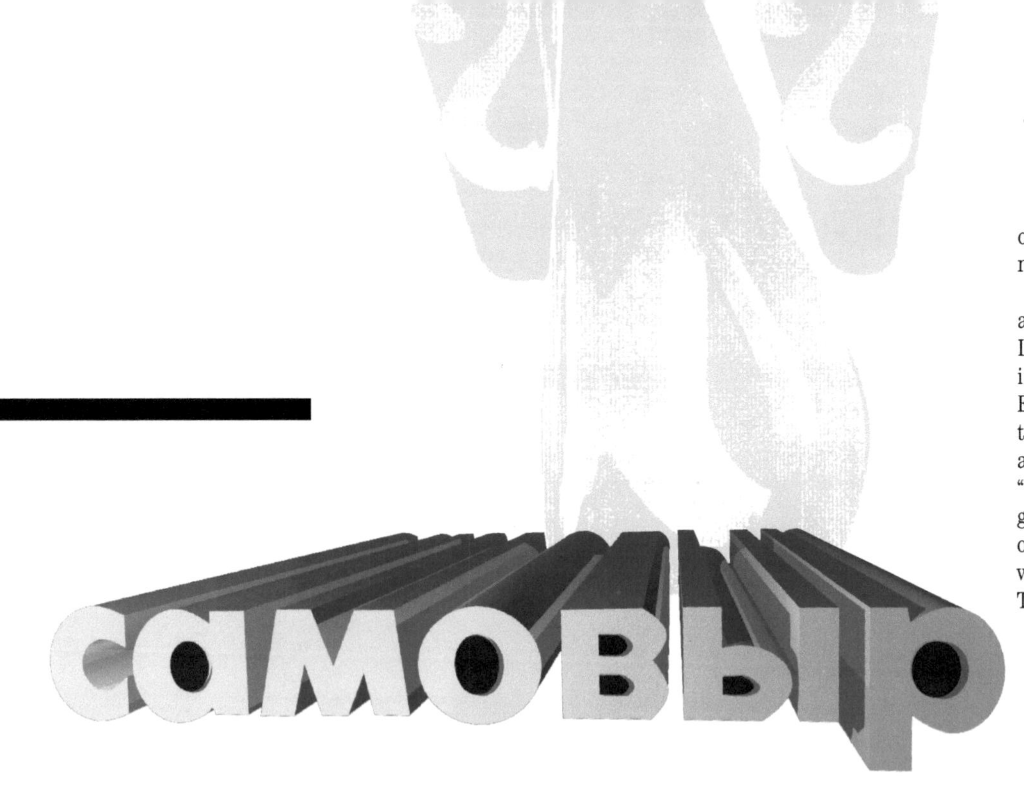

isn't so much a romanticised review as a glance into the toolbox of the everyday media.

Eastern Europe Watching

One of the first lessons to be learned as the Iron Curtain rose was that the Eastern bloc was hardly a bloc at all in the sense of a homogeneous whole. Various mentalities and various socialisms had been brought together under red flags large and small which waved more for the big brother than for their siblings. Distance, and often a deep scepticism, separated the countries of the Warsaw Pact. In 1985, the Hungarian author György Dalos described a few of the reasons for the differences between the small central and Eastern European nations: "Their religious backgrounds are different: Catholic, Protestant, Russian Orthodox and Islamic traditions live next to each other and the historical experiences are not any less divergent. There are countries in which tremendous revolutions occurred in the nineteenth century (Hungary, Poland); there are those where none have occurred (Romania, Czechoslovakia). A few of the countries in the region have mixed populations (Romania, the Soviet Union), and in others, national minorities are insignificant. The overall picture is further politically differentiated according to whether the individual countries were allies of Nazi Germany during the Second World War or were members of the anti-fascist coalition. Besides these past differences, or those which can be attributed to the past, there are those that derive from the current situation in the individual countries. Among these are size, economic strength, the level of consumerism, the role of the public, freedom of movement, etc."[1]

Slavoj Zizek, psychoanalyst and student of Lacan, upon whose couch in Ljubljana the New Europe lies, formulates the situation in terms of a common question: "Who will be 'let in', integrated into the developed capitalist order, and who will be shut out?". The qualifying principle is a frightening one: "Each player in this bloody game of collapse attempts to legitimise its place 'within' by presenting itself as the last bastion of European civilisation (the current shorthand for the capitalist 'within') against Oriental barbarism"[2]. Zizek has compared this process to the game 'Who's It' where absolution for one means condemnation for another, and described a postmodern variant of it being played in East Germany, Poland, Hungary, Slovakia, etc. – one based, ultimately, on the 'relative' nature of borders: "... For the Croatians, this all-important border is naturally the one between them and the Serbs, that is, the one between western Catholic civilisation and the Eastern Orthodox collective spirit which cannot fathom the values of western individualism. [...] the Serbs believe they are the last line of defence for Christian Europe against the fundamentalist danger embodied by the Islamic Albanians and Bosnians."[3]

The heterogeneity of the (homogeneously named) Eastern Bloc could also be found in the plethora of varying media maps – a transparency and translucency of borders, not only to the West but also within the East, dependent on whose signals you were receiving. Czechs were checking out Polish news programmes, Hungarians were watching Romanian football, Romanians peeping into Yugoslavian movie broadcasts. Besides the national television stations and the official papers which, as Karl Schlögel notes, were just as thin everywhere with the same bad photos and the same chemically sanitised articles, the international Western radio stations with their much wider broadcast area, such as the BBC World Service or the Deutsche Welle, played an extremely important

Czechs were checking out Polish news programmes, Hungarians were watching Romanian football, Romanians peeping into Yugoslavian movie broadcasts.

role in the distribution of news and discussions which were not reported by the state media of Eastern Europe. Of overwhelming importance was the U.S. Radio Free Europe which, from its base in Munich, was received in all central and Eastern Europe as a dissidents' broadcaster and mouthpiece of the American standpoint during the Cold War.

And of course, on the local level there was an abundance of small unofficial and niche media which were often short-lived and yet maintained an exchange of information and communication which, according to the official version, could not exist. Records and audio cassettes as well as jokes passed on by word of mouth – Radio Eriwan! – traced maps, and endlessly circulating copies of books were just as effective and meaningful. In countries where no private use of photocopying equipment was allowed under any circumstances, a multitude of illegal publication strategies for the distribution of ideas were invented, most of which were referred to by the umbrella term Samisdat. A related principle was *ramka*, which was originally Polish but then spread to Hungary and elsewhere. Miklos Haraszti writes: "The *ramka* in the East is the equivalent of the photocopier in the West. The recipe for *ramka* goes like this: Soviet power minus electrification. By the way, this cross of silk screen and offset printer can be built in two hours at home – and is capable of several thousand impressions. There are times when the police, like worrisome gardeners, mow down the boldly sprouting Samisdat to the roots. But the *ramka* is ineradicable. *Ramka* is virtual freedom of the press; he with the fingers smeared black with ink, the human rights professional, points to the free, electronic future"[4]. In these times of electronic networking, we should not forget that a hand press can have a practical dignity which the internet, with its susceptibility to control, will never attain.

Ramka is virtual freedom of the press; he with the fingers smeared black with ink, the human rights professional, points to the free, electronic future

Soluble History

Each of the central and Eastern European 'revolutions' in the eighties has its own history and series of events in each country: From the Polish 'interruptus' to the aborted Russian perestroika and the Hungarian slippage to the capitalist goulash, the abrupt collapse of the East German regime to the brutal Romanian Christmas story. In the Baltics, it was song, in Prague, softspoken words, in Berlin, candles and bad shoes that rang in the new era.

Although it's clear now in retrospect that there was a certain logic in the developments of the late eighties, from Gorbachev's perestroika, the political liberalisation in Hungary and Poland to the occupation of the West German embassy in Prague and Warsaw by East German citizens in the summer of 1989, the events that late autumn came in a form which was more or less unexpected. The Western media were all over these events, or rather, they wanted to be.

The result was a blanket of suspenseful media spectacles that went on for weeks – we even forgave the live media the endless repetition of the same video footage. It was here that life was happening, here that history was happening right in front of our eyes. And not just for Western television viewers, but also and especially for the people in the countries themselves, the medium of television was serving an important catalytic function. For weeks, the people of Leipzig watched their Monday marches on Western television and went out on the streets in even greater numbers the following week. At the symposium "The Media are with us!", held as early as April 1990 in Budapest, the art critic Magda Carneci said of the role of television in the Romanian revolution: "Television wasn't simply a giant, tireless eye that continuously beamed the absolutely irrepressible images, but it also served as something of a collective brain: It received, selected and distributed news throughout the whole nation which was utterly essential for the coordination and upholding of the fighting spirit (...) In a certain way, television justified the revolution for most people."[5]

A short time later, the revolutionary reality, in the light of the great number of competing authentic documents of the collective experience, naturally ran up against doubt. Hardly four months after the events in December, Carneci remarked: "Since the first days of the revolution, things have rapidly changed. What one sees now on television about the Romanian revolution is becoming, it seems to me, more and more a fiction."[6] Similar adjustments occurred in East Germany and in Czechoslovakia where competing versions of the history circulated and called the victory

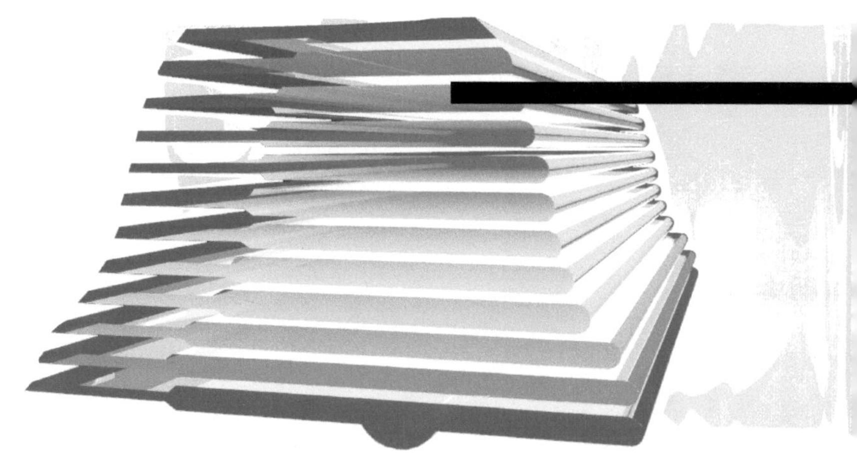

of the little revolutionaries in the street into question. A contradictory complexity was being revealed, especially as journalists ceaselessly continued their search for new 'fact'

For the West, there was the additional difficulty of distilling ways to deal with all that had been gathered by the media. While the good guys and the bad guys were still clearly distinguishable in 1989, and hence an optimistic look into the future was all that was required, the Western perception of the war in Yugoslavia from 1992 onward was considerably less sure of itself. But how can a politically and historically complex story be packed into three and a half minutes? And while historians and military strategists quarrelled over the formulas for understanding and intervention, the media created a perception of a declining slope which would force action. But the media achieved the opposite and the reports on the war in the Balkans led to paralysis in Western observers instead of the will to intervene. The media triumph of 1989, when the media could make history, met its Verdun in Dubrovnik, Srebrenica, Gorazde and Sarajevo, where it couldn't prevent history from happening.

'Open Society' and 'New World Order'

The absurdity of Fukuyama's notion of the 'end of history', an idea which seemed to some almost tangible in 1989, was made all the more blatant by the sudden 'return of history'. And yet – the short moment between the supposed zero hour of history and theunexpected 'entry into the present'[7] briefly revealed an astounding piece of theatre. In the fall of 1989, the Australian media critic McKenzie Wark followed the events in Europe through his television: "One thinks of Europe in 1989 as the opening night at the theatre where the curtain goes up and the audience comes face to face – with another audience. One has to be outside the theatre altogether to see the whole thing together as one big spectacular show."[8] The Western public had followed the revolutions of 1989 with enthusiasm, but the object of the fascinated gaze was not just the rediscovery of democracy as such: Those in the West are all too well aware of the shortcomings and cul-de-sacs of real, existing liberal democracy to be fascinated by it. But, as Zizek's Slovenian colleague Rado Riha writes, the encounter was a re-discovery of self: "In the assumed fascination with democracy of the Eastern Europeans, the Westerner could see himself in his 'pure' form, not yet tainted by empirical disillusion and false steps, and grasp the untarnished origin of his democratic being."[9]

Strengthened by the supposedly naive gaze from the East onto the fascinating West, actors of the most varied of stripes (sects, banks, parties, private set ups and non-governmental organisations [NGOs]) began a race to see who would be the first to bless the East. The 'new world order' proclaimed by George Bush at the end of the eighties found its first expression in the occupation of the East by ideological pioneers. In Croatia alone, 790 representatives of international or regional NGOs are currently witness to an unbelievable boom in the private sector. At present, the vacuum left by the retreat of the state and public supervision in many post-socialist countries of Eastern Europe is being filled by the unregulated activities of NGOs.

One of Eastern Europe's most important and influential NGO is the Soros Foundation for an Open Society, created by the Hungarian-American multimillionaire and philanthropist George Soros. Besides its other humanitarian engagements, this foundation is particularly involved in the creation and support of independent media (for example, Radio Zid in Sarajevo, *Arkzin* in Zagreb, Radio B92 in Belgrade, the daily newspaper *Koha Joone* in Albania, as well as internet and email communication). With its high-profile support of new Eastern European democracy movements, the Soros Foundation has earned itself a highly contested reputation. Its success in filling the vacuum of public and private sector support has not always won it favour with respective governments. By the same token, considerable sums of money are circulating which are subject to neither democratic control nor any form of governmental regulation. John Horvath has described the use of the ISF as, "a means for shrewd market penetration in an economically prostrate region" and questions to what extent the NGO can be seen as building a "Soros-controlled telecommunications empire".[10]

Critical Technology

Informal networks, newsgroups and internet mailing lists which are often used by hundreds of people to keep in contact and exchange news and discussions play a significant role in the spreading of critical information. The significance of this provokes the question of whether technology is normative for cultural and social behaviour and in what way it has unifying effects on this behaviour. And if the introduction of technology – and the immanently unifying or 'normative' tendencies of translocal technologies – leads to a dissolution of cultural differences or hinders specific local means of expression. Can technology be 'culturally neutral' at all? Or – and this was asked at a symposium in Prague in December 1996 – "Does media art imply [a] kind of thinking which is West-oriented and linear, masculine, etc.?" Prompting, from Bratislava, Martin Sperka's equally challenging retort: "So, feminist thinking is East-oriented and non-linear?"

The 'new world order' proclaimed by George Bush at the end of the eighties found its first expression in the occupation of the East by ideological pioneers

The meaning of media cultural practice is not only technological and translocal in nature, but also constantly unfolds in local contexts. A careful look at local cultures and local codes is therefore urgently required. Various artists from Eastern Europe have repeatedly referred to the meaning of the always disrupted relationship to 'the media'. The Albanian artist Eduard Muka said in an interview in 1996: "We inherited a sort of hatred towards the media. There were a lot of lies, nothing was exact, there was only propaganda. Still there is only one state television channel and it is even worse than it used to be. The distrust towards media could be a good starting point for artists to make their critical approach in regards to media. I look at media as the highest degree of manipulation humanity has ever invented. In this sense, this could be really used to raise social or individual imperatives."[11]

Going East, Going West

Travelling in Europe is still difficult but is becoming simpler and more normal. The borders are more porous, even if visa matters and language differences still hinder the movement of people, goods and ideas. The obstacles are gradually diminishing and a rediscovery of a (not exclusively historical) cultural space in Europe is beginning.

Seen cynically, cities such as Sarajevo, Moscow and Tirana have been the unrecognised cultural capitals of Europe for years (which other European cities are turned into media images this often?) But why are Albania, the 'Balkans', Russia, Chechnya, etc., covered so thoroughly by the media? Certainly not because they are 'normal' parts of Europe, but rather because they maximise the production of media reports. The bloodier it is, the more mass media (especially television) can report live on extraordinary situations. The media image of Eastern Europe has been characterised by extraordinary situations; normality is hardly ever communicated.

The importance of the 'small media' on the other hand is that they, unlike 'big media', are able to convey something of 'normality' and to make understanding possible. The 'small stories' offer an alternative to the 'grand narratives'. This is what we call the small media normality for the East.

Berlin, April 1997

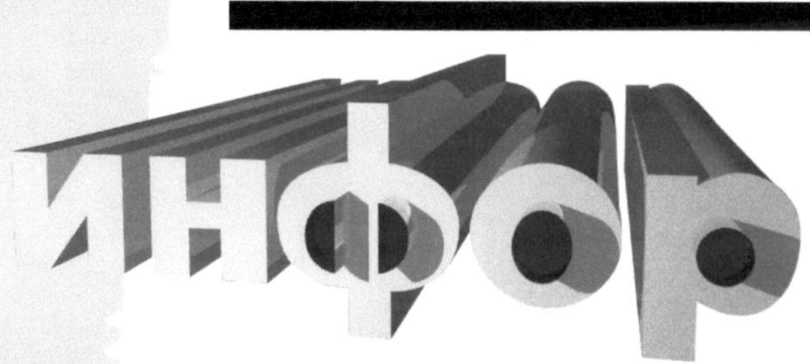

[translated by David Hudson, Berlin]

An extended version of this text – *Small Media Normality for the East* – was published in • P. Schultz / D. McCarty / G. Lovink / V. Cosic (eds.), *ZK Proceedings 4: Beauty and the East; Ljubljana: Digital Media Lab, 1997,* pp. 17-21 and on *Rewired – The Journal of a Strained Net,* June 9-15, 1997 [*www.rewired.com*]

[1] *Kursbuch 81*, Berlin 1985, p. 4
[2] Slavoj Zizek, "The Malaise in Liberal Democracy", in *Heaven Sent*, No.5, Frankfurt/M., 1992, pp. 47 - 48
[3] Ibid., pp. 47 - 48
[4] *Kursbuch 81*, Berlin, 1985, p. 31
[5] Peter Weibel (ed), *Von der Bürokratie zur Telekratie. Rumänien im Fernsehen*, Berlin, Merve, 1990, pp. 19 - 21
[6] Ibid., p. 22
[7] Karl Schlögel, *Go East oder Die zweite Entdeckung des Ostens*, Berlin, Siedler, 1995, p. 9
[8] McKenzie Wark, *Virtual Geography. Living with global media events*, Bloomington, Indiana UP, 1994, p.60
[9] Rado Riha, *Reale Geschehnisse der Freiheit. Zur Kritik der Urteilskraft in Lacanscher Absicht*, WO ES WAR 3, Vienna, Turia & Kant, 1993, pp. 14 - 15
[10] John Horvath, "The Soros Network", Nettime mailing list, Feb. 7, 1997 and *Telepolis* Journal [www.heise.de/tp], Jan. 31, 1997
[11] Eduard Muka, Interview with Geert Lovink, "Media Art in Albania, First Steps", Syndicate mailing list, Sept. 29, 1996

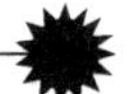

Inke Arns **X**inke@berlin.snafu.de**X** is a curator and organiser of several media art exhibitions: OSTranie 93 (Bauhaus, Dessau); Medienbiennale Leipzig 94; discord. sabotage of realities (Kunstverein Hamburg 1996/97).
Andreas Broeckmann **X**abroeck@v2.nl**X** works with V2 Organisation Rotterdam and is the moderator of the V2_East/Syndicate mailing list.

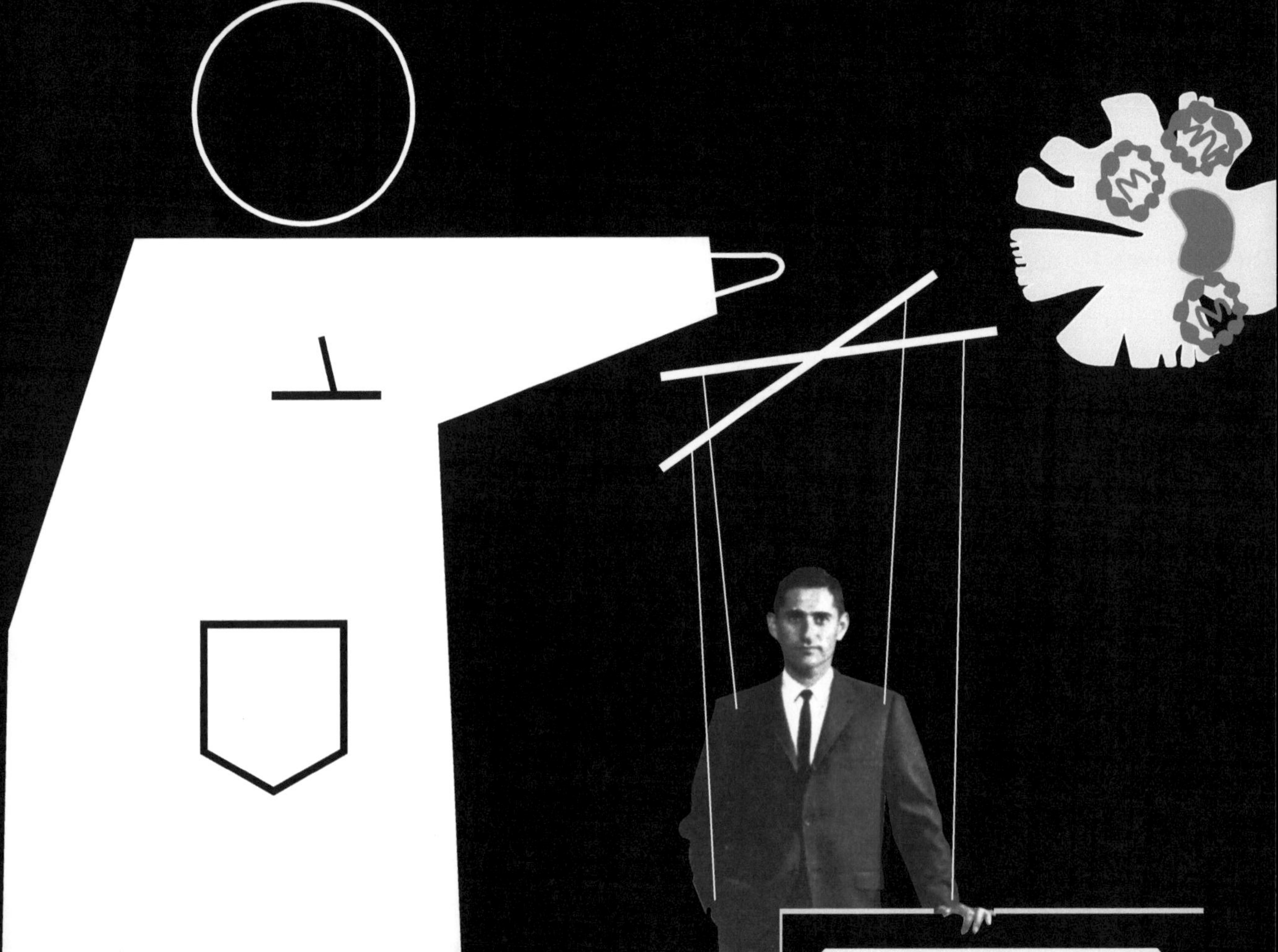

The Biotech industry "now rivals the oil industry for weight and influence" says Rob Cummins, the director of the Pure Food campaign. This quote, taken from a four day special report in *The Guardian* newspaper, is typical of the recent swelter of media-speculation on the industry's growing power. The Labour government's moratorium on the introduction of genetically modified foods has brought to the boil a debate which has long simmered in the public psyche. After ploughing hundreds of billions of pounds into research, the American dominated 'agri-business' is too close to payback time to be put off by a handful of 'resistant Europeans'. After all, Europe is potentially the world's second largest market for their product range.

It is becoming an all too common revelation to hear of 'independent' government advisors, even critics, also holding down jobs on the boards of

TECHNOLOGY CONSENSUS CENSUS
Mute interviews Richard Sclove of the Loka Institute about corporate accountability and the state of technological democracies.

IN MALAYSIA: CYBERCOLONIALISM
Never knowingly undersold... PM Mahathir's Hollywood style business-planning is proving a bitter pill for Malaysian citizens. While attempts are made to expatriate 1 million foreign workers and the economic crisis deepens, the fate of Mahathir's pet project – the Multimedia Supercorridor – seems uncertain. John Hutnyk on Science Cities.

QUESTIONNAIRE
Mute contributes to Europe's research data-mountain with an unauthorised picture of Technoscience. A selective sample of consumer feeling on genetic engineering, hi-tech pharming and modern medical institutions.

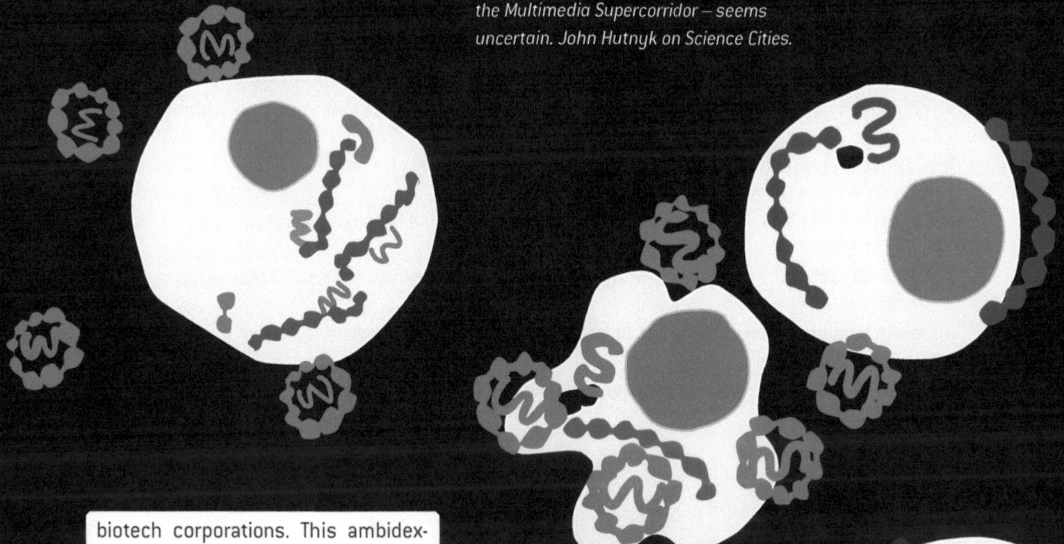

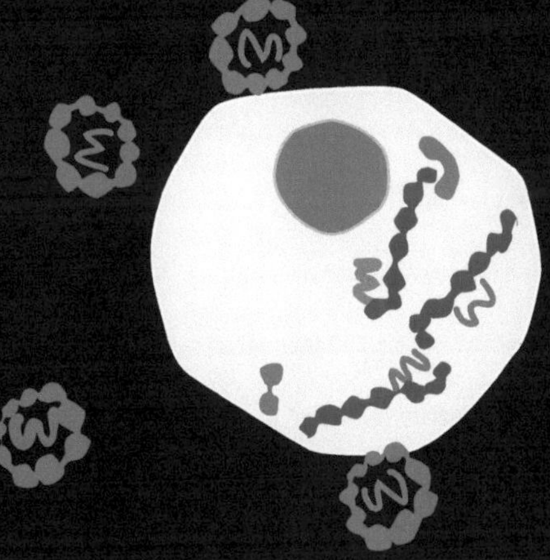

biotech corporations. This ambidextrous career strategy can only deepen the existing discrepancy between the industry's hi-finance PR and lobbying campaign and the absence of a powerful, independent critical force. The corporate takeover of agriculture, the collapse of biodiversity, and the unpredictable results of letting engineered life forms 'into the wild' are just a handful of the doubts surrounding the biological revolution. But to be cautious does not imply a lemming like return to the illusory bosom of Big Mamma Nature.

This summer, *Mute* spent ten days at Kassel's Documenta-X exhibition, participating in the Hybrid WorkSpace (see *Mute* 8, Short/Cuts). During this time, we explored the theme of Technoscience with invited guests (Kate Rich/BIT, Armin Medosch and Manu Luksch, Kathleen Rogers and Rob La Frenais, John Hutnyk, Krystian Woznicki and Josephine Bosma). Technoscience is the intersection point of the information and life sciences, where the technological marries the living in a bid to conquer death and disease, endow life with the utility of technology and technology with the kiss of life. The fact that Technoscience spans more than its trademarked products (OncoMouse, Dolly, bovine growth hormone, the Flavr Savr tomato, IVF) was one of the project's leitmotifs – its economic dimension becomes the real Surgeon General presiding over the birth of this technoscientific progeny.

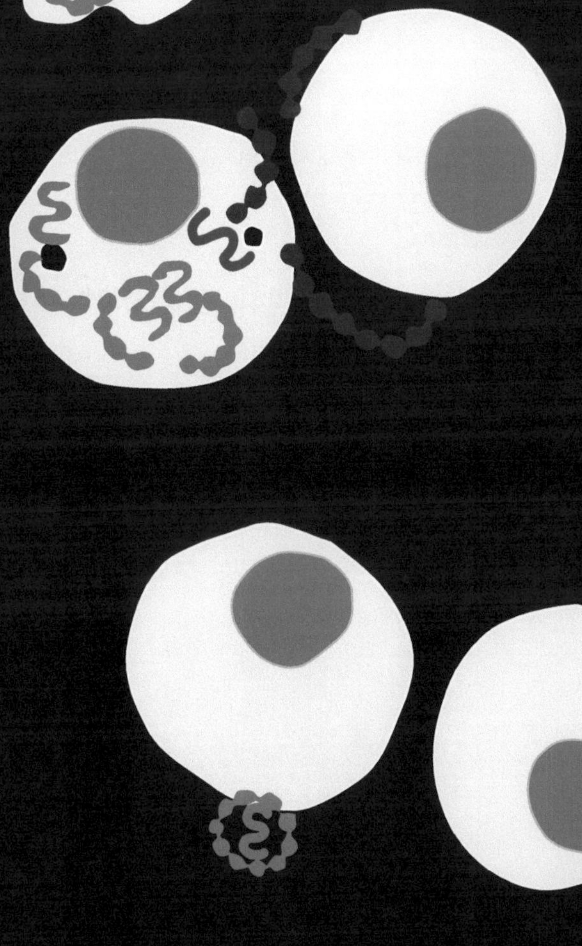

Why is it that our politicians seem to have developed an aversion to debating certain subjects – and we're not just talking sleaze? Squeamish issues like the introduction of gene patenting or the genetic manipulation of animals are debated at length in private, and yet get only very few public airings if compared to the micro-dissections of each new budget. Though no more or less difficult to grasp hold of than a system as complex as the economy, we, the electorate, are under the collective delusion that these matters are over our heads and best left in the hands of the experts. And those experts are as impartial as only captains of industry and research scientists can be. So why have we relinquished our control over the introduction of certain scientific and technological developments into our society, and what is being done to resist this institutionalised passivity? *Mute* interviewed the Loka Institute's founder and director, Richard Sclove.

TECHNOLOGY CONSENSUS CENSUS

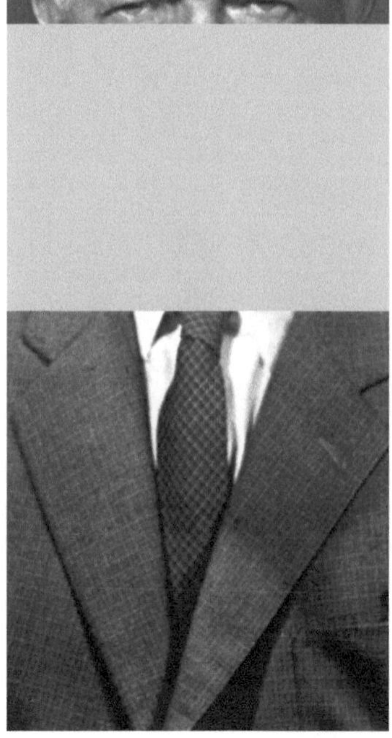

M: I'd like to start by asking you a bit about the work of the Loka Institute.

RS: The Loka Institute is a non-governmental organisation based in Massachusetts in the United States, studying and calling attention to the social effects of technology. We do advocacy work and organise the development of new participatory institutions to get a wider range of people participating in decisions about science and technology.

M: What successes have you had so far?

RS: We haven't succeeded completely with anything, but the two institutions with which we've made most headway are modelled on European institutions. One is a variant of what in Europe are called 'science shops' that are most fully developed in the Netherlands. These are institutions to which universities direct some of their research in response to questions raised by public interest groups, grassroots organisations, trade unions and local government agencies. So it's a way of having universities conducting research not just for industry, intellectual curiosity or for the government but also for other sectors of society.

In the US we call them 'community research centres' because the Dutch word 'science' doesn't distinguish between natural and social sciences. It's often the case in the Dutch science shops that their studies involve everything from, say, environmental toxicology work to studies for a women's group in Amsterdam. They wanted to know if there would be a market for an independent women's radio station. In the US we found there already were a certain number of organisations who did community based research. The main difference is that in the Netherlands basically every Dutch university has one to ten of these community research centres. And they are networked with each other. Originally this was just by telephone and newsletter, these days it's with the internet, and they're networked with each other in a way that if a community group wants research assistance on a social change project they can go to any one of the science shops and they will be referred to any one of the centres that has the kind of expertise they're looking for. So in the Netherlands, they have a comprehensive system that can basically address any community oriented concern on any topic coming from anywhere in the country.

M: So what you are saying is that in the States the existing research centres were randomly distributed and working independently of each other?

RS: Absolutely, their distribution is very accidental. And they haven't even been aware of each other's existence. So the first thing that we've done is to make these existing programmes and centres in the US aware of one another and begin to develop a capability to learn from one another, to make references and be more visible and accessible.

M: Is the internet really helping to encourage that kind of activity?

RS: It is. I don't say that as an unqualified supporter of or enthusiast about the internet, as I spend a lot of my time talking about its potential downsides, but yeah, in this case it has helped a great deal. I mean, when I first started writing about this I published an article in a conventional newspaper and then on the internet, and the conventional newspaper got me one or two phone calls and the internet distribution quickly yielded 300 people who said, "yeah, I want to work with you on this".

M: Well, it's certainly how we found you.

RS: We found that the existing centres and programmes in the US are excited to find out about each other's existence and are generally quite eager to work with us on building a network. The challenge is as always to find funding to support this effort. (laughs)

M: Are you getting any state funding for your work?

RS: Very limited. But not zero in my case. We happen to be based physically in Massachusetts and our state-wide extension service which is government supported has contributed some financial support to this effort.

M: Now I wonder whether I can ask you a bit about why you've chosen the subject of science and technology to focus on people's lack of influence within the decision making process, as opposed to the multitude of other issues that also affect us. For instance our defence policy. Why is that any different in a democratic system where we elect representatives and at that point waive our own individual say in those issues?

RS: Well, it's actually not very different from the military issue, but I'd say the military and the science and technology issues together are different from most others.

M: Why is that?

RS: There are probably several reasons why I focus on science and technology issues. I don't do it because I think they are the most important issues in the world. I think they're up there, but I think there are lots of important social concerns about ordinary housing issues and welfare and medical issues. So it's not that I think that it's the most important. But among important issues, it is one that gets the very narrowest public representation or participation. For instance, (I know the US case best, because that's where I live) in the US our democracy is imperfect in many respects. But I'd say there's more imperfection in how science and technology decisions are made than in many others. For instance, we elect representatives to our congress in the US, but then we don't assume that they just do their own thing. We also assume that they are responsive once they're elected to various popular social concerns. Now in most issues, like education, or health policy, even though it's imperfect, there is some sort of public interest or community representation. In congressional deliberations, for example. Business lobbying may typically have a disproportionate say, but there is

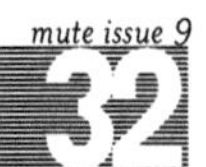
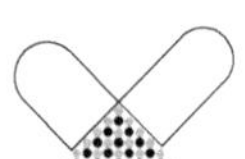

going to be some kind of public interest or community voice or representation...

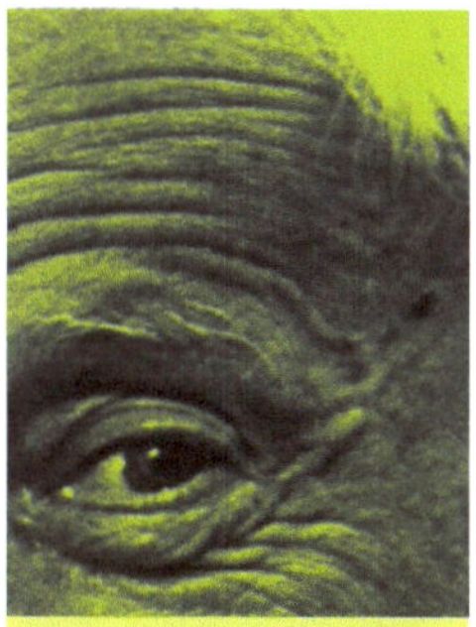

M: And you would say that was based on the ease with which the lay person can understand issues to do with welfare, for instance, or housing, as opposed to the exclusive language of science?

RS: That's a piece of it, but that's not the whole of it. In science and technology policy making, our congress is influenced pretty much exclusively by representatives of three groups which are: business, the military and élite academic researchers. Nobody else has a voice and yes, the argument that those three groups would make is that of course they should make those decisions because first of all, they take the broad public interest to heart and are good representatives of it and secondly other people, they claim, wouldn't understand these issues and wouldn't want to participate.

M: How do you practically see the possibility of translating the complexity of scientific ideas and language into a language that the pubic can understand in all its subtleties, so that they're then equipped to make a valid judgement?

RS: Right, if there were more time I'd answer that in a few ways, but I should probably just talk to you about why I'm in Denmark rather than talking to you from the US.

M: Maybe you could answer that question through the practical example of Denmark.

RS: The Danish government has really made strides in developing new participatory institutions that address exactly that concern. One of them is something they call the consensus conference, which has been done about 15 times over the last 10 years in Denmark, and since then maybe half a dozen times in other European countries. The process is a little bit like a jury in a court. If the Danish government is going to be debating a complicated, controversial question like biotechnology policy or how we should make use of knowledge from the Human Genome Project, their Board of Technology – which is where I'm currently working – assemble a jury (as it were) of about 15 quasi-randomly selected Danish citizens. The panel excludes anybody with expertise on the topic and it excludes anybody from an organised interest group that is active.

M: How are those people actually found?

RS: They've done it differently in different countries. The way they do it in Denmark is advertising in local newspapers. When we did the first one of these as a pilot test in the US last April we did it through random phone calling. In any of these you

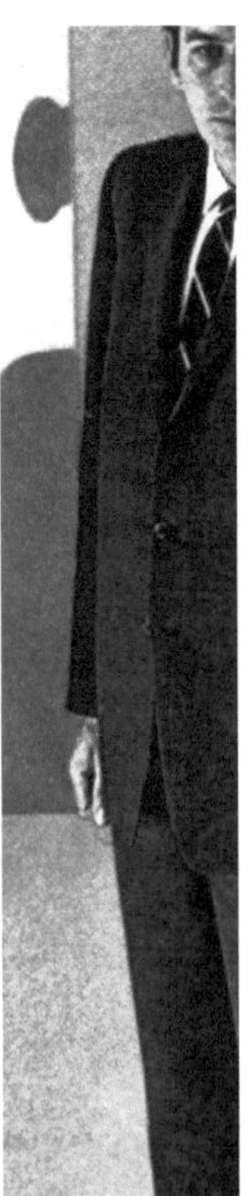

assemble a steering committee that oversees the whole process. A steering committee is composed of knowledgeable representatives from groups that do have a stake in the issue. Some would be from industry, some from academia, some might be from public interest groups.

M: And there's no danger of the steering committee putting pressure on the elected panel based on their own interests?

RS: Well, there would be that danger. The way, if you do it properly, and the way they appear to do it in Denmark is if you pick that steering committee, it should be a balanced group who counterbalance each other. The one time something of this kind was done in the UK, that was not done, and the steering committee had precisely some of that biased impact you're referring to. Not that they directly influenced the lay panel, but I think they influenced the materials and experts that the lay panel interacted with.

M: I see. And they're there to really explain the issues, explain the material?

RS: Not the steering committee. Because the steering committee is actually balanced against itself, they assure some reasonable impartiality to the process. But the process is that the lay panel spend two weekends being brought up to speed a little bit on the process. They review some material that the steering committee agrees are not biased wildly one way or the other, and maybe would not meet with experts, in the Danish case. But if, for instance, they're doing something on biotechnology they might meet with a high school teacher who explains to them a little bit about DNA, and they might meet with a journalist who explains a little bit about the political terrain of the issue and who the actors are. Then they have a three or four day public forum, after the lay public has been brought up to speed on the issues, that takes place in Denmark in the parliament building. And there anyone in the public or media who's interested can sit in while a group of experts (that the steering committee has approved as not being biased) take turns testifying in front of the lay panel. Then the lay panel takes turns cross examining them. Finally the experts are all dismissed and the lay panel writes up a report drawing their own policy conclusions on the question.

M: And what sort of impact do those decisions, that as far as I understand are not then turned directly into legislation, have on the way that policy is decided or the way that industry then decides to back certain kinds of practices and research and not others? Have there been any positive examples of that?

RS: Yes, in Denmark where it's been done the most and where it's become most institutionalised there are demonstrable impacts. They don't, as you said, become law and I don't think anybody believes they should because it's a very small group and it's not adequately representative of the whole society. It's a way of getting an informed, diverse lay perspective into deliberations, but you don't want it to determine those deliberations.

In Denmark, they did a conference on food irradiation in 1989 and that influenced the parliament to ban irradiated food in Denmark, except in the case of dried spices. They did one on the use of knowledge from the Human Genome Project and that influenced the parliament to place strict controls and limits on the use of genetic screening information on insurance and hiring decisions in the work place. And there's some evidence anecdotally that it has, without going through the policy channels of the industry, some influence on industry. Industry in Denmark was initially resistant or sceptical to the process for the same reasons you'd expect it to be in most places. But over time, because these processes occur in the early stages of the development of a piece of technology before a lot of money has been invested by industry, it actually gives them political foresight that can be very useful to their own bottom line considerations.

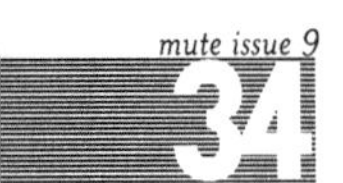

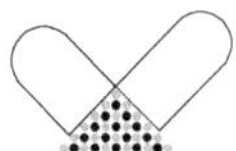

M: So it's like a very early feedback source.

RS: Yes. For instance, the opposite of that was in the US, where the Monsanto Corporation, about ten years ago spent 300 million dollars developing something called Bovine Growth Hormone to artificially stimulate cows' milk production. As soon as that was brought to the market it turned out that small farms and many consumers opposed it. But because Monsanto had no public input at early stages and had already sunk 300 million dollars, they fought like crazy to make sure that this thing went to the market whether consumers wanted it or not.

M: How do you see the shift during this century from industrial technologies to information technologies? Do you see any positive developments in that change?

RS: Yes and no. I see no positive developments in the uncritical, one-sided enthusiastic hype about IT being a panacea that's going to solve all kinds of social problems. That hype is quite dangerous because these are complex technologies, and any implementation of them will have good and bad effects. But some implementations will still be better than others. The hype just conceals those choices that need to be made, and allows industry to make them without public participation. So the hype is bad. As for the technologies themselves, I'm quite ambivalent.

M: But the net is clearly a cheap way for you to challenge the information monopoly of the large corporations....

RS: Loka is a small NGO, we function like many such organisations on a very insecure shoestring budget, always in danger of going under financially. We are basically challenging dominant institutions and forces by arguing for democratising decisions that existing powerful institutions like controlling. For that reason it's hard to get resources to do what we do, and that's one of the reasons that we do a lot of our work on the internet. It's not that I intrinsically love the internet. Given that these issues are politically very under developed (there's not a long history in the US of people thinking about how to broaden representation and participation in technology issues, and there's not a lot of money to work on the issue either) I have often chosen to do what I would call preaching to the predisposed-to-be-converted. After very little persuasion they become allies. So I haven't engaged that much with industry because I'm busy doing something else.

M: You take the example of the Amish to discuss the sophistication with which certain societies handle the inclusion and exclusion of technologies. Why did you choose the Amish as an example? I am especially interested to know how you think that you can apply such a model, derived from a very small and closed society, to a comparatively vast and heterogeneous society such as the USA's?

RS: There are a couple of reasons. It's not that I uphold them as an ideal society, but with respect to decisions about the introduction of technology and their social effects the Amish are the experts. And what's interesting about that is that the strictest old order Amish in the States, of which there are about over a hundred thousand in some 25 states, prohibit formal education past the age of fourteen. So they have this population that by conventional standards is very uneducated in school-based ways. And the standard argument in our society is that lay people can't participate in these decisions about technology because if you don't have a PhD in mechanical engineering or biology you can't understand them. Yet what is fascinating about the Amish (who are popularly seen as being anti-technology because for instance they still use horses a lot) is that they still use a lot of modern technology, but very selectively. They will, for instance, use tractors, but not for what they were intended. They'll use horses for ploughing and will sometimes own tractors, but put them into neutral and drive them around the farm and use them as a mobile source of mechanical power to do other things. What's fascinating is the way they make the decisions. They do all sorts of, upon reflection, real obvious things that we don't. Like it's real hard to predict the social effects of a technology, so one of the things they do is put new technologies that they're curious about on probation for a year. They say, anyone who wants to adopt it for a year can do it, but we're going to watch what happens to us as a result and re-evaluate at the end of a year, and if we think that it's not having a bad effect we'll continue allowing people to use it. And if, after evaluating it, they conclude that it's having a bad effect then they won't use it. That's a simple empirical test that we don't do. We do it for drugs. We sort of won't allow new medical, pharmaceutical products onto the market until we've tested them for their medical effects. But we'll allow any technology, no matter how upsetting its social and political consequences, out there if it makes a profit.

M: I suppose there with the Amish, the question is: how is their decision making process structured? Is there any real opportunity for political dissent?

RS: I'm not putting the Amish up on a pedestal, in the sense that regardless of what the answer to that was, what's interesting from my point of view is the fact that these people, who don't educate themselves past fourteen in schools, can still make very sophisticated evaluations of technology's social effects. Even if you felt that they did that in an undemocratic way.

M: Do you feel that small initiatives like yours can have an affect in a culture which, in comparison, has introduced technologies in a far less thoughtful way?

RS: I would say that in absolute terms LOKA hasn't had that much affect, and yet our affect has really been disproportionate to the time we've existed on our resources. We already have roughly 7000 people on our internet list serves world wide and a considerable international following. But we're at too early a stage to know how much headway we can make.

Richard Sclove was interviewed in August '97 by Pauline van Mourik Broekman and Josephine Berry during *Mute*'s Technoscience slot at the Hybrid Workspace. Sclove was in Denmark at the time, working for the Danish parliament's Board of Technology as a visiting researcher. Sclove is also the author of *Democracy and Technology*, New York/London, Guildford Press.

[www.amherst.edu/~loka] and email: **X**Loka@amherst.edu**X**

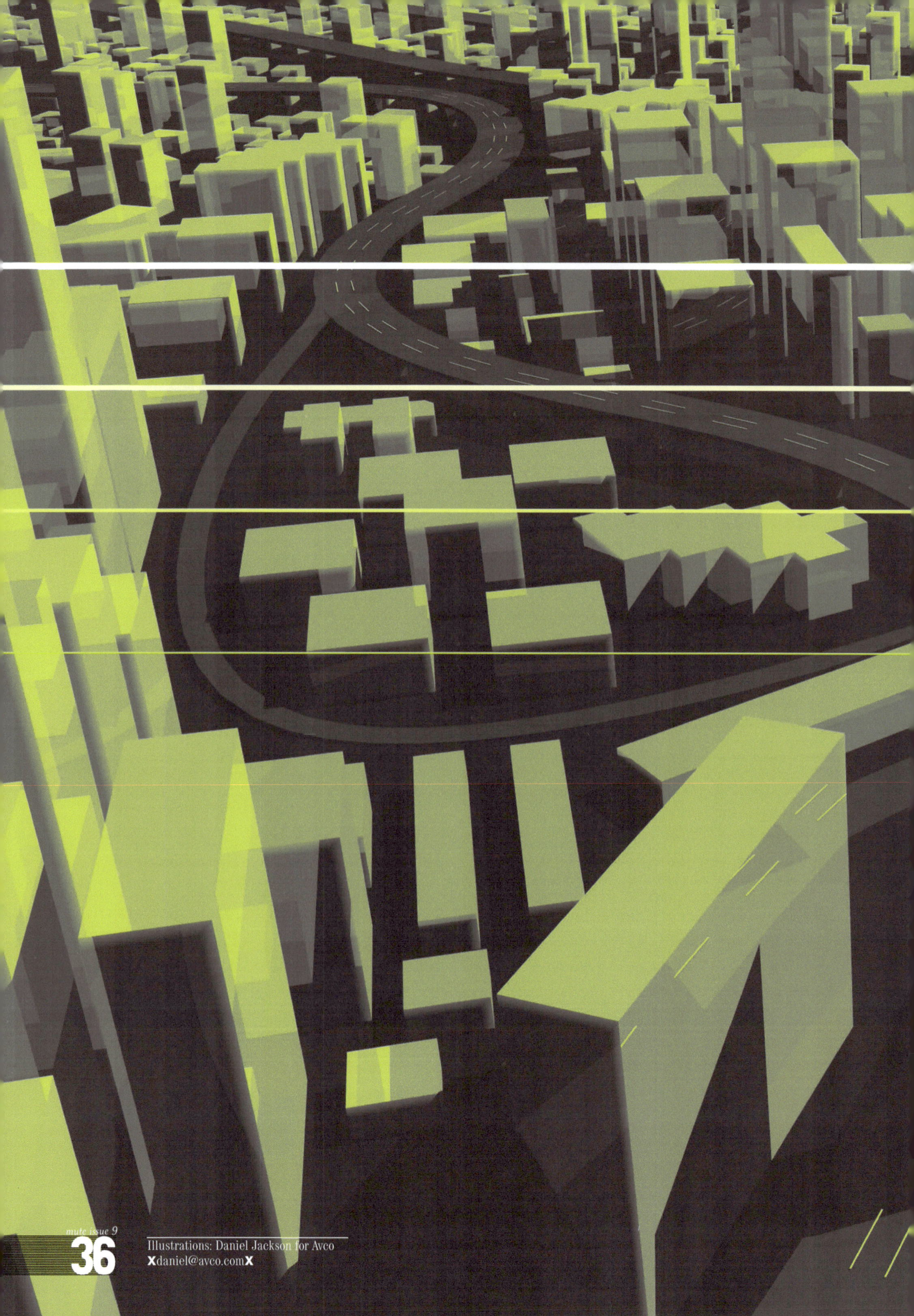

Illustrations: Daniel Jackson for Avco
Xdaniel@avco.comX

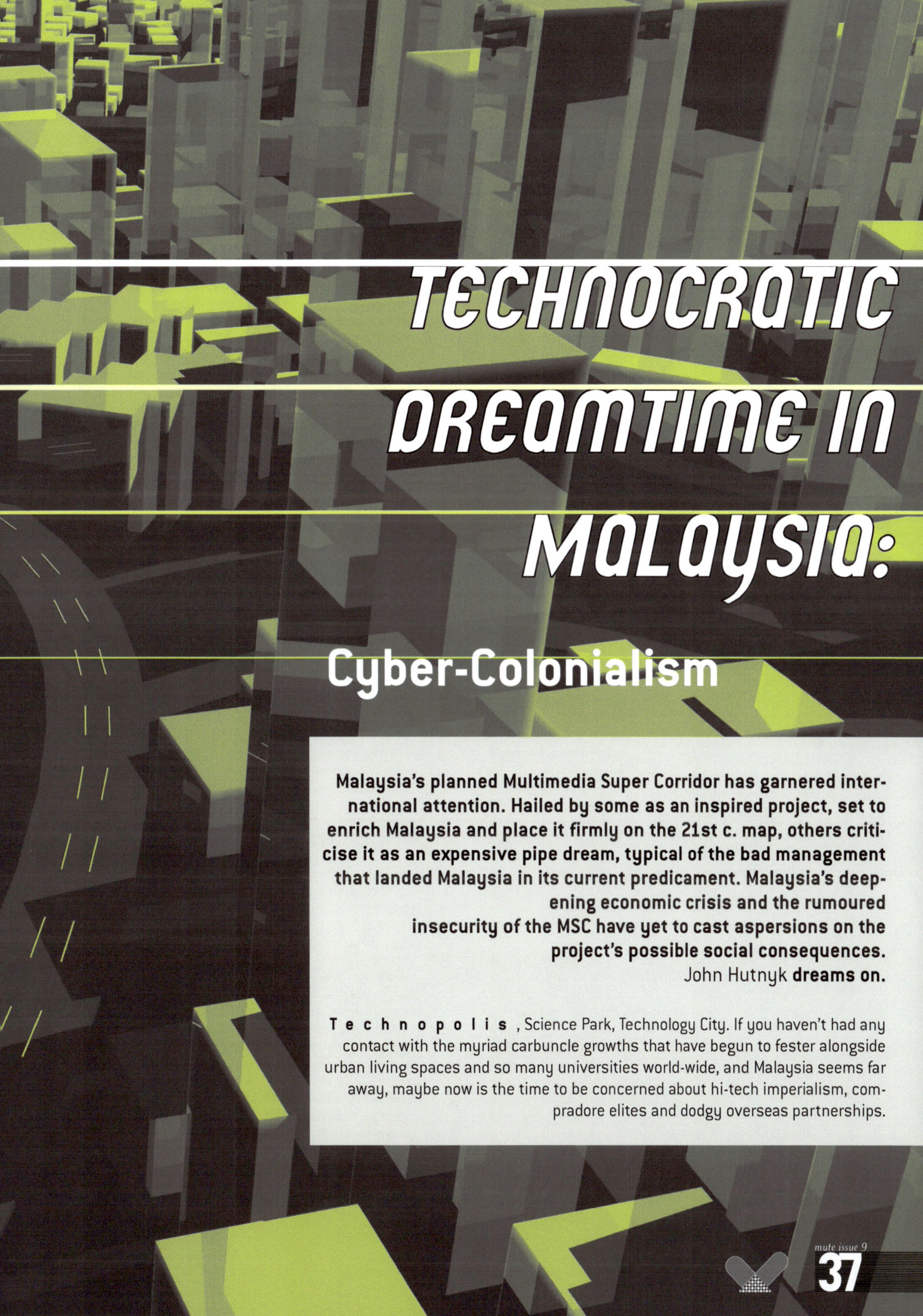

TECHNOCRATIC DREAMTIME IN MALAYSIA:

Cyber-Colonialism

Malaysia's planned Multimedia Super Corridor has garnered international attention. Hailed by some as an inspired project, set to enrich Malaysia and place it firmly on the 21st c. map, others criticise it as an expensive pipe dream, typical of the bad management that landed Malaysia in its current predicament. Malaysia's deepening economic crisis and the rumoured insecurity of the MSC have yet to cast aspersions on the project's possible social consequences.
John Hutnyk **dreams on.**

Technopolis, Science Park, Technology City. If you haven't had any contact with the myriad carbuncle growths that have begun to fester alongside urban living spaces and so many universities world-wide, and Malaysia seems far away, maybe now is the time to be concerned about hi-tech imperialism, compradore elites and dodgy overseas partnerships.

Prime Minister Datuk Seri Dr Mahathir bin Mohamad was recently prevented by a virus from a planned visit to the UK to sell the future, and in Kuala Lumpur a few hiccups in monetary policy have clouded the horizon, but the dreaming schemes of hyper-modernity have been touring the world – LA, Tokyo, Berlin – and the future seems very close indeed. The 'Multimedia Super Corridor'™ is only a construction contract away.

The MSC has always been an international project. At the beginning of 1997 a cabal of the 'great minds'[1] met with Mahathir in a specially convened 'Advisory Panel' in Los Angeles, USA, to flesh out the flashy proposals that may transform Kuala Lumpur's skyline, and construction industry cash flows, once again. The great minds included CEO's and Directors of multinational corporations such as Siemens, Netscape, Motorola, Sony, Compaq, Sun, IBM and more. The Chancellor's Professor of UCLA was there, and Bill Gates was invited (though couldn't make it in the end). The discussion was no doubt convivial.

What was under consideration at this talk-fest for which the PM and his offsiders had come to LA, was an integrated hi-tech development project designed to make Kuala Lumpur and surrounds – a fifteen by fifty kilometre zone south of the city – the information hub of South East Asia. Trumpet headlines announced the future in the Times, the Star and the Sun. PM's speeches and supporting echoes from Ministers proclaimed that the MSC project would "harmonise our entire country with the global forces shaping the information age"[2]. Such harmonisation with the orchestration of the multinational info-corps makes for singing praises in the press. The headlines scream: "Global Bridge to the Information Age", "MSC immensely powerful, unique" and "PM's Visit to US Triggers Excitement". Big dreams indeed. Even the pop-electronic fanzine *Wired* got in on the buzz and called the project, quite favourably it seems, "Xanadu for Nerds"[3].

In this context, success of a Science City is initially about confidence – the importance of hype. Here, the future can seem very fragile indeed.

But what exactly is to be in this Multimedia Super Corridor; what are the serious prospects for its success, and by what criteria should it be assessed? The promotional material, as can be expected, does not spare the hype:

"Malaysia's Multimedia Super Corridor (MSC) is a bold initiative – a regional launch site for companies developing or using leading multimedia technologies. Aiming to revolutionise how the world does business, the MSC will unlock multimedia's full potential by integrating ground-breaking cyberlaws and outstanding information infrastructure in an attractive physical environment."[4]

The key parts of the proposal include a series of research and development 'clusters', basically science labs and info-technology factories, located near a new airport and a 'cybercity' including state of the art condos, shopping complexes and transportation facilities, in a secure (everyone must carry an electronic 'National Multipurpose identity Card') and 'attractive' garden city. Telemedicine, Electronic Government and full ("uncensored") internet connectivity are also touted. All this overseen by the twin Advisory bodies of the Multimedia Development Corporation – they put up the web site – and the Advisory Panel of the 'great minds'.

Why did the first MSC promotion meeting take place in Beverly Hills? Well, obviously the internet and international connectivity of the grand scale to attract the likes of Gates (Microsoft) and Gerstner (IBM) is not there in Kuala Lumpur yet. Similarly, PM Mahathir went direct from LA to Japan for another parallel hi-level corporate luncheon. The point is to attract investment, or rather tenants, for the research laboratories that will be built. One does not want an empty corridor, so one travels to where the clients are. An open invitation.

But what is the invitation to? The development of Science City ventures such as this is not a new idea, though it has become something of a craze since the first versions of the concept of integrated science city living were spawned out of the heads of the planners at Japan's MITI. Engineering new Silicon Valleys has become the grand vision of subsequent planners from 'Silicon Glen' in Scotland, to the Multi-function Polis in Adelaide. Not always successfully, the more than 300 plus of such ventures compete for relatively rare technology research pay-offs, as the cutting edge of such research is closely guarded and nurtured by the wealthy mega-corps. In this context, success of a Science City is initially about confidence – the importance of hype. Here, the future can seem very fragile indeed. From the beginning of the year when the Prime Minister was talking up the '2020 Vision' with super conferences in Hollywood, to the CNN televised roller-coaster of the virtual market stock exchange troubles, it's been a dynamic time for futures in Malaysia.

The 2020 Vision "has been delayed", Mahathir was forced to announce, as speculative capital became more tentative and the projects which formed the core of the vision of achieving 'Developed Nation status' in 23 years were put on hold. The complex repercussions of the slide of the Malaysian Ringitt and other stocks, along with controversies over projects such as the Bakun Hydroelectric dam in Sarawak, and 'the Haze' problem afflicting the region, have clouded projections and predictions. Development and profitability seem less secure than before; the tallest building (twin towers Petronas), the biggest airport, the longest office, the undersea electricity cable and the Cyber-Malaysia Multimedia Super Corridor now all appear as costly monuments (whether completed, stalled or abandoned) to the precarious gamble of speculative development within very late capitalism. Of all the new big projects that marked Mahathir's Malaysia as the go-ahead new tiger-cub of South East Asia, only the MSC project, and related services attractive to international R&D such as the airport, have survived the imposed austerities of the currency crisis. Confidence and hype require more than big buildings and upbeat reviews on CNN.

Thus, the questions that have to be asked about technological research-generated development are multiple. The first questions might include a consideration of the parameters of the new Science City fad and, in the context of worldwide restructuring, the impact on regional communities in the zones where such cities are planned. The impact upon those now employed in an increasingly narrowing and exploitative manufacturing sector, let alone those from the agricultural sector whose lands are bought up for condos etc., is likely to be profound. It is no doubt they who will soon gain part-time and casual employment as ancillary workers and service personnel in these hi-tech fantasy enclaves and semi-standard accommodations alongside them no doubt. Starting with questions about impact upon people – possibly still an unusual approach in development discussions – is worthwhile as it reminds us that what should be asked is: what does Malaysia get out of such a development? Malaysia as yet does not have the infrastructure or ready local expertise – in terms of university graduates – to fill the labs to the scale of the envisioned dreamscape, and so presumably, Malaysian employment in the corridor is to be of the service type. Well, indeed, at first a flurry of construction activity – and the concomitant exploitation of migrant labourers and subsequent racism – but in the end, jobs as cleaners and porters in the corridors of Info-Tech.

Who will be the hi-tech workers? A layer of technocrats and experts will need to be recruited, from in part the expat Malaysian elites schooled in the salons of Stanford, MIT, London and Manchester, but in large part, at least in the first phases, the already existing personnel of the multinational infocorps that are invited to 'relocate' will provide staff for the most important posts. The imported workers will have expat lives and an expat status which is not far from the old 'colonial career' that has always been the hallmark of business empires under imperialism. These appointments will have several corresponding run-on effects. In this context consideration of the impact of recent technological innovation in the old metropoles upon those now engaged in the (neo)colonial manufacturing enclaves and the Special Economic Zones etc., is required as a part of any assessment of tech-driven extension of exploitation in the 'off-shore' production sites of South East Asia. Given the range of projects abandoned in the wake of the Ringitt crisis, why is it that PM Mahathir's dream is to go for the hi-tech option instead of extending manufacturing for the local satellite regional economies (surely sales of medium level manufactured goods to ASEAN partners holds strategic economic merit)? Is the hi-tech only gambit not likely to open still further the path of super profits and speculative super exploitation? A less stark, but nevertheless important, question is why the Special Export Zone option with the tax breaks, cheap labour, low shipping excises etc. is no longer the preferred path, and is instead replaced by a risky corridor venture chasing the possibility of 'technology transfer' and rapid transit to a Bill Gates-sponsored cyber-future? The problem is that the conditions for such transfer are not quite worked out and there is nothing to really entice the key parts of such corporations to the KL Corridor, nor are the generous tax concessions, infrastructure developments and other State funded inducements calculated to lock-in technology transfer in a way that Malaysia could exploit long term.

What, and who, after all is the MSC for? Is it again a project to make the elites rich, and one which does not contribute, except perhaps through the vagaries of trickle-down theory and a vicarious, somewhat quixotic, reflected glory which allows the Malaysian people to take pride in Mahathir's international notoriety? Or can it be demonstrated that the old international imperial production modes are magically reversed by the MSC, rather than continued in new format? Where once jungles were cleared for plantations, where these plantations were then cleared for condos and shopping malls (which lie empty or underused) and where the manufacturing sector was geared largely for export rather than ever for use or need, can it be that the multimedia development will somehow restore productive capacity to local priorities? Is multimedia the key to local content, local uses, local needs, or even to regional variants of these same priorities – the very priorities that we have too often learnt are always second to the goal of profitability, and which seem increasingly subject to the fluctuations and constraints of international competition? The 'people's' interest in the trade in shares, the speculation on futures and the infrastructure development company extractions, are all based on some future pay-off which does not arrive, or at the least does not arrive for the majority of Malaysians. Of course there are a small few who have always benefited from exploitation of the country's economic efforts – be they the plantation owners, the condo contractors, or the new 'big project' development engineers. The problem is that instead of moving towards a more adequate mode of production, given regional and local conditions, possibilities and necessities, those setting the direction of economic activity in Malaysia seem to favour older selective benefit structures and priorities. There is no indication that a leap forward into the MSC is likely to disrupt existing feudal discrepancies of income, lifestyle or quality of life. Here the contradiction is the same one as that between colonial masters and peasant labour, such that we might name as semi-feudal, cyber-colonial that situation where the most advanced technological capacities will benefit old social hierarchic formations which refuse to budge.

But let us not dismiss the project of technology transmission too quickly. Questions about the criteria which would make Hi Tech City developments successful, or at least a worthwhile gamble, must be put up for discussion. The usual considerations here are more to do with the culture of technology development under capitalism in general and do not account for the particularities of the international division of labour and power. Yet these aspects deserve to be thought through. Some of the questions include such generalities as: how might technological innovation be best achieved and what are the requirements for 'synergy' – the concept such projects use for optimal mix of infrastructure support, creative personnel, 'attractive' environmental factors and the 'spark' that ignites ideas and innovations? Similarly, how does one plan for creativity and the celebrated 'milieu of innovation' that are the buzzword ambitions of these sci-fi enclaves? What is the preferred mix of government public sector, private industry and university support? What regional and historical factors come in to play in determining the suitability of such developments in either previously industrialised centres of

The imported workers will have expat lives and an expat status which is not far from the old 'colonial career' that has always been the hallmark of business empires under imperialism.

long standing, or in newly emergent capitalist economies? How do political and economic contingencies impinge upon the long-term prospects of innovation? What are the policy requirements? (for example how restrictive are local intellectual property and patents guidelines?) Is it all just a fantasy built upon a few otherwise unpredictable successes (Silicon Valley, Cambridge, Munich)? Is technopoly a passing fad?

But surely those that have holdings in construction could just keep on making money out of condos, dams, hotels and roads, and so all this info and multimedia stuff is too risky speculation?

What then are the conditions of take-off for Mahathir's proposed dreamscape? The prospects for synergy and innovative creative hyper invention rely upon the relocation of corporate R&D which is less than likely to arrive. The 'milieu of innovation' that fuels the successful ventures of this kind does not yet seem to exist in the Malaysian plan – though there certainly is the fab idea in the proposal to build a 'cyber-versity'. The international division of labour, the agendas and opportunisms of the neo-imperialist world order, the short term interests of monopoly capital and the inability to provide a lock-on to capital and technology which may relocate to Malaysia are not, none of them, addressed in the promotional or planning literature. There are very real obstacles which would need to be solved if any technology project were to succeed in the East Asian sphere. Given that Gates has said that Microsoft will not shift its 'fundamental' research outside the USA, it is not a grand prospect. The realities of the international economy do not favour such projects outside the already entrenched centres. The cost to the Malaysian state, and so therefore the public purse, is likely to be greater than that which can be recouped in the short or long term.

At the risk of inviting the wrath of the 'recalcitrant' PM, we could ask a different series of questions, ones that would be less generous, but not less plausible in their speculations: for starters, who will profit from the development of the MSC? Do Prime Minister Mahathir and his cronies, the elites and supporters of the good news propaganda in the press, have capital invested in the multimedia transnationals that may locate in the MSC corridor? If Malaysian elite capital is attached to Bill Gates' capital, then perhaps the MSC makes sense for them, if not it is just a corridor crying out (perhaps in vain) for Gates' profiteering. Or alternately, do PM Mahathir and other members of the Malaysian elite have capital tied up in the construction industry? This we know is the case from the controversy around the company Ekran and its now stalled plans to build the Bakun hydroelectrical dam in Sarawak (flooding the homes of 10,000 Orang Ulu peoples, and creating more than sufficient energy to run Malaysia, as well as an additional smelter or two – see Australian corporate miner Comalco's plans to process aluminium in the region – via a bizarre undersea submarine electricity cable joining the two halves of the country). But surely those that have holdings in construction could just keep on making money out of condos, dams, hotels and roads, and so all this info and multimedia stuff is too risky speculation? Why go for this hi-teck bizzo? Isn't building factories and warehouses for off-shore assembly and export processing profitable enough? Is the writing on the wall in that sector – and does it say build corridors not factories, the end of manufacturing profit is nigh? Or, considering the most cynical case, will this Super Corridor actually have anything in it? – or is it just a flash way of selling more construction (with corresponding bribes and kickbacks etc.)? Even if the R&D firms were to locate some of their lower level R&D in the corridor, how long would it stay – hi-tech production is very short on shelf life, and very mobile in terms of set ups (I bet you the labs they made Office 97 in at Microsoft were fitted out differently than the ones for Windows 95, new partitions in the veal-fattening pens and so on, new posters on the walls, new cartoons pinned to the noticeboards). What is the prognosis for the economics of the project if even these simple questions are so obvious? Surely better analysts than us have seen that the gains are not there. What are the justifications? I suspect the recent fluctuations of the share market indicate where the problems lie – this is a virtual, rather than actual, development and 2020 is a very long way off. Once upon a time the strategy of compradore elites was to profit primarily from State subsidised local industrialisation and development, or at best plantations and resource extraction, within their own national domains. This did at least have the benefit of advancing national and local industry, although it would be necessary to quarrel with the direction, ownership and benefits of that industry. The sorry history of elite wealth extraction is second only to that perpetrated by imperialism. Subsequently, however, and largely in the face of the internationalisation of the neo-colonial capitalist market, through mergers, buy-outs and centralisation, it is more often the strategy of such elites to attach whatever capital they may have to other successful capitals – say those of a Gates – and profit from whichever short-term option, anywhere in the world, offers the best return for large mobile capitals. In this situation there is thus no lock-in to industrialisation for any particular site, and the capital invested accumulates increasing capacity to exploit and appropriate wherever it can best, so that even to the detriment and cost of the citizens of any particular national elite. Increasingly it becomes necessary for compradore Governments to make local resources – people, land, power – available at the cheapest possible rates so as to attract capital investment for even the shortest periods.

What factors would ensure the success of the MSC? Given that the MSC comes as a late entrant in the chase for the techno-grail, lessons for Malaysia might be drawn from the experience of other similar ventures and maybe Mahathir can profit from that experience. Maybe. In a study by Manuel Castells and Peter Hall – called *Technopoles of the World*[5], 1994 – it is possible to glean some criteria: the question of Government support is shown to be crucial as no such development can really succeed without considerable concessions and grants from a supportive administration. National, State and Regional Governments providing administrative and infrastructure assistance to corporate sector clients fosters an attractive environment for Capital. From the point of view of Corporate industry it is eminently agreeable that many of the associated costs and burdens of new product

John Hutnyk is the author of *The Rumour of Calcutta: tourism, charity and the poverty of representation*, Zed Books, London
xJohn.Hutnyk@urz.uni-heidelberg.dex

generation and development be facilitated under Government subsidies – and so Malaysian taxpayers' cash is thrown into the corridor leading to pearly launch vehicle of information heaven – the necessary costs of production in individual cases are here deferred onto the public purse. Similarly, the support of adjacent higher education institutions is shown to be important as a stock of researchers are thereby kept on the public payroll, and although often superseded in terms of equipment, labs and so on, as the technology city grows, the availability of university laboratories and libraries is a convenient and again public facility. This all the more so, if the researchers are mobile and contract – imported – intellectual labour as well. The scenario is fast looking like another bungled rip-off since other factors like transport, roads, tollways, vehicle pollution and land given over to car-parking, and refuelling, repairing, services, as well as the infrastructural side issues of support provision in the form of everything from legal and secretarial services, cafes, housing, shopping and recreational factors – including cleaning, nursing, childminding and even sexual services would also become necessarily available on the new tekno estates that would serve, in order to appeal, those that might locate on an 'attractive' science-tekno-hyper-cyber-future-city.

Splendid to see. There are many language tricks that transmute this dreamscape into a sales pitch for short term gain. Mahathir's sparkling prose notwithstanding: he said in his introductory speech that the MSC would entail "the careful creation of a region with an environment especially crafted to meet the needs of leading edge companies seeking to reap the rewards of the Information Age in Asia", and so the prospects for the Multimedia Super Corridor look promising only to those poised to move in an make a fast buck. The corridor is just as likely to become a conduit for neo-colonial business-as-usual as it is to deliver the promises as promised. Who is going to build it if not the migrant workers that are so ill treated in Malaysia, and for that matter world-wide? Who is going to service it, if not the casual and part-time workers that are so badly remunerated, both in Malaysia and world-wide? Who... The good news keeps on coming, Mahathir emphasises the point in another well constructed turn of phrase: "I see the MSC as a global facilitator of the Information Age, a carefully constructed mechanism to enable mutual enrichment of companies and countries using leading technologies and the borderless world".

A borderless globe of profit making opportunity is not fun either for luddites or for those who see this only as another trick played across the international labour and prosperity divide. There is definitely a hype in the air, and this needs to be taken seriously, the forging ahead rhetoric envisions the prospect of development and prosperity, and the plans are up for weighty 'great minds' type discussion. Indeed, that's why there is a global Advisory Panel willing to offer advice and a 'critical' apparatus ready to do the fine tuning to introduce the momentous transformations that these tekno-dreamscapes represent. "They broke their backs lifting Moloch to heaven" (Allen Ginsberg, Howl, 1956)... The future is going to come true.

1 *New Straits Times*, 18th January, 1997
2 Prime Minister M. Mahathir's speech in Los Angeles, 14th January, 1997, from the special web page advertising the project – [www.mdc.com.my/msc]
3 Greenwald, *Wired*, issue 5.08 August, 1997
4 MSC webpage [www.mdc.com.my/msc]
5 Castells, Manual and Hall, Peter, *Technopoles of the World: The Making of 21st Century Industrial Complexes*, Routledge, London, 1994.

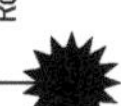

November 1997

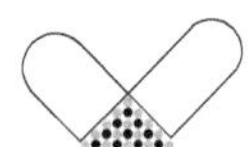

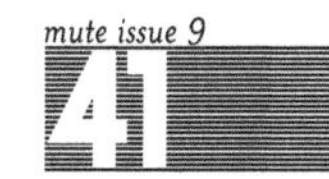

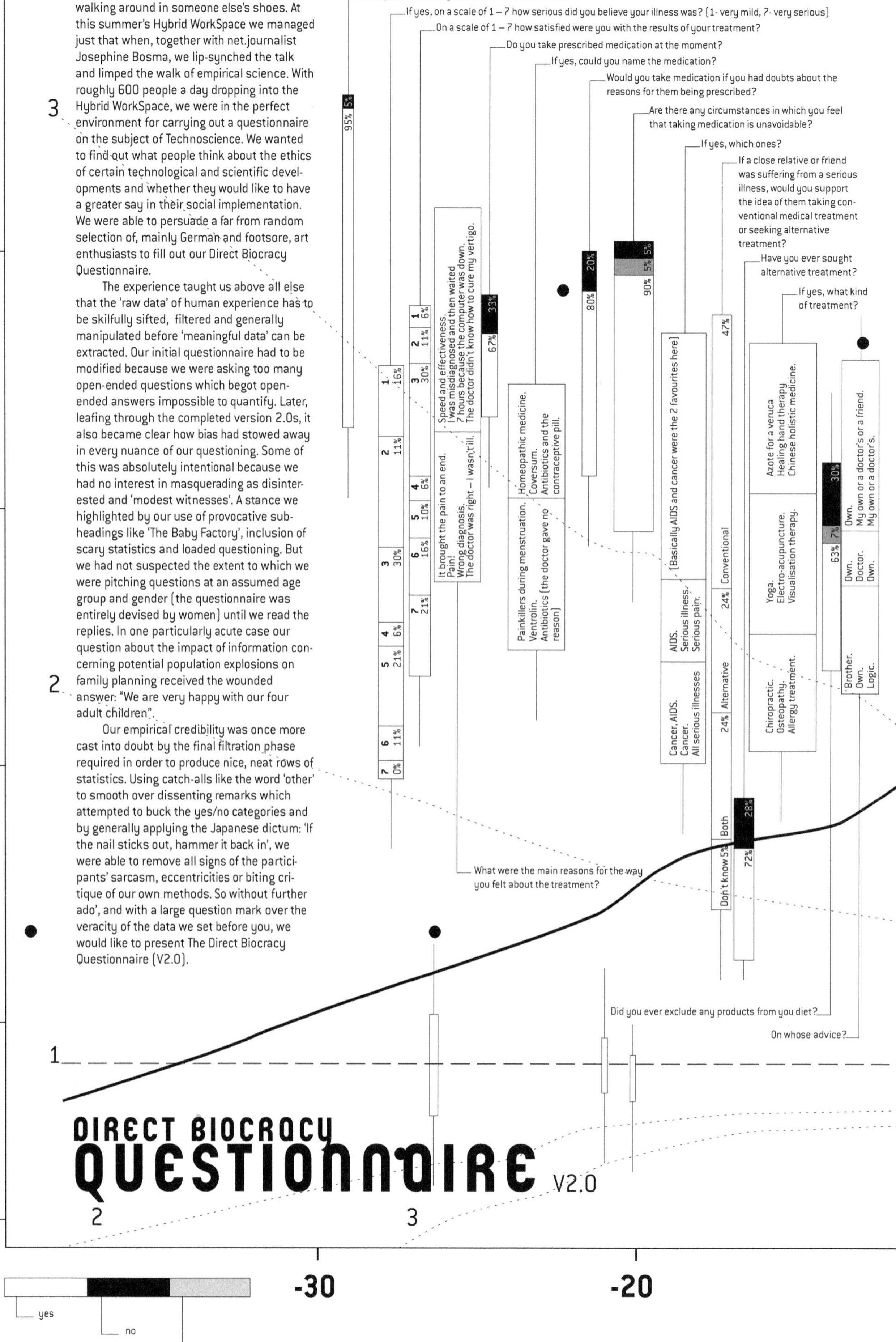

If you want to develop blisters try walking around in someone else's shoes. At this summer's Hybrid WorkSpace we managed just that when, together with net.journalist Josephine Bosma, we lip-synched the talk and limped the walk of empirical science. With roughly 600 people a day dropping into the Hybrid WorkSpace, we were in the perfect environment for carrying out a questionnaire on the subject of Technoscience. We wanted to find out what people think about the ethics of certain technological and scientific developments and whether they would like to have a greater say in their social implementation. We were able to persuade a far from random selection of, mainly German and footsore, art enthusiasts to fill out our Direct Biocracy Questionnaire.

The experience taught us above all else that the 'raw data' of human experience has to be skilfully sifted, filtered and generally manipulated before 'meaningful data' can be extracted. Our initial questionnaire had to be modified because we were asking too many open-ended questions which begot open-ended answers impossible to quantify. Later, leafing through the completed version 2.0s, it also became clear how bias had stowed away in every nuance of our questioning. Some of this was absolutely intentional because we had no interest in masquerading as disinterested and 'modest witnesses'. A stance we highlighted by our use of provocative subheadings like 'The Baby Factory', inclusion of scary statistics and loaded questioning. But we had not suspected the extent to which we were pitching questions at an assumed age group and gender (the questionnaire was entirely devised by women) until we read the replies. In one particularly acute case our question about the impact of information concerning potential population explosions on family planning received the wounded answer: "We are very happy with our four adult children".

Our empirical credibility was once more cast into doubt by the final filtration phase required in order to produce nice, neat rows of statistics. Using catch-alls like the word 'other' to smooth over dissenting remarks which attempted to buck the yes/no categories and by generally applying the Japanese dictum: 'If the nail sticks out, hammer it back in', we were able to remove all signs of the participants' sarcasm, eccentricities or biting critique of our own methods. So without further ado', and with a large question mark over the veracity of the data we set before you, we would like to present The Direct Biocracy Questionnaire (V2.0).

DIRECT BIOCRACY QUESTIONNAIRE V2.0

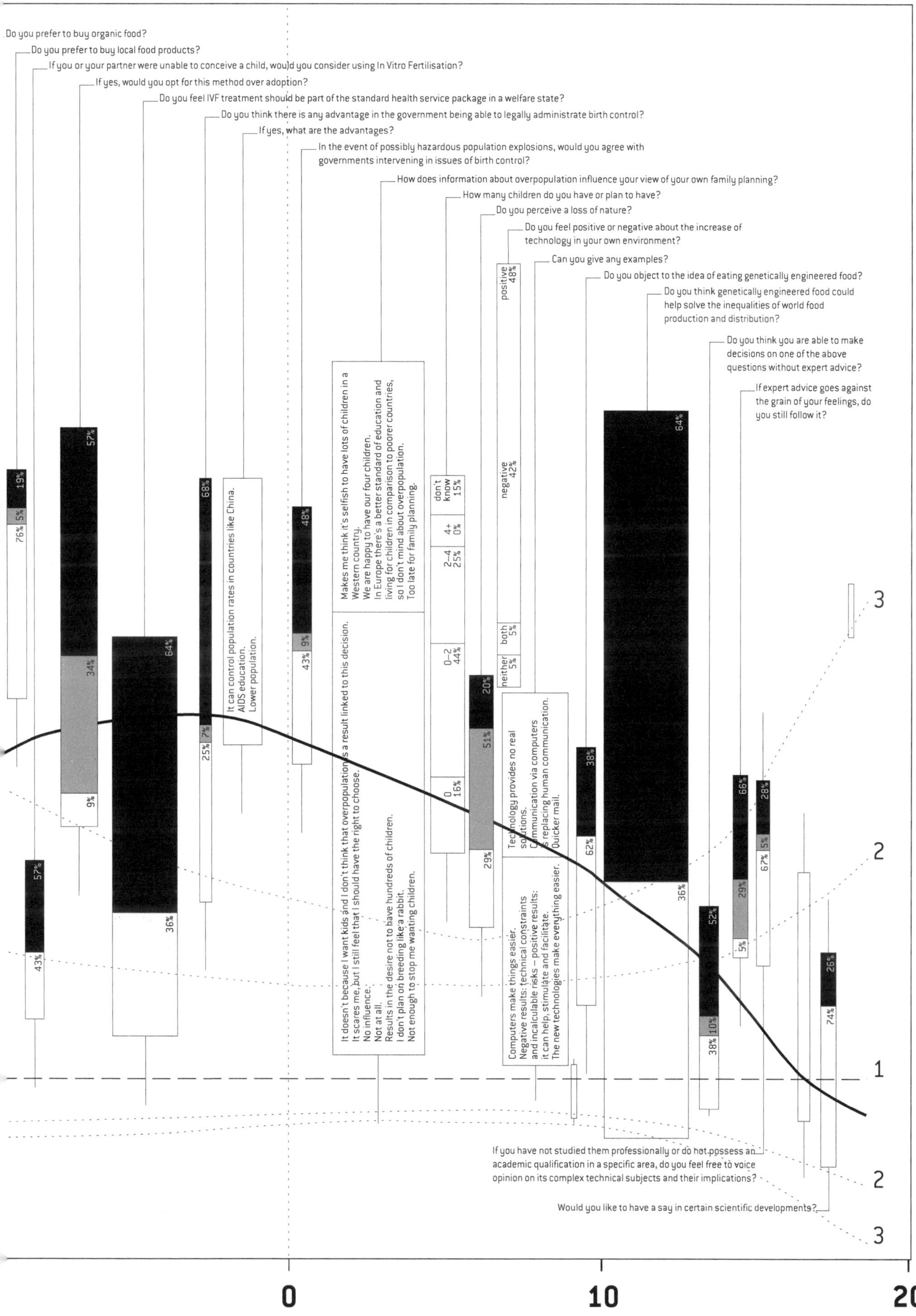

Do you prefer to buy organic food?

Do you prefer to buy local food products?

If you or your partner were unable to conceive a child, would you consider using In Vitro Fertilisation?

If yes, would you opt for this method over adoption?

Do you feel IVF treatment should be part of the standard health service package in a welfare state?

Do you think there is any advantage in the government being able to legally administrate birth control?

If yes, what are the advantages?

In the event of possibly hazardous population explosions, would you agree with governments intervening in issues of birth control?

How does information about overpopulation influence your view of your own family planning?

How many children do you have or plan to have?

Do you perceive a loss of nature?

Do you feel positive or negative about the increase of technology in your own environment?

Can you give any examples?

Do you object to the idea of eating genetically engineered food?

Do you think genetically engineered food could help solve the inequalities of world food production and distribution?

Do you think you are able to make decisions on one of the above questions without expert advice?

If expert advice goes against the grain of your feelings, do you still follow it?

19% 5% 76%

57% 43%

57% 34% 9%

64% 36%

68% 7% 25%

It can control population rates in countries like China.
AIDS education.
Lower population.

48% 9% 43%

Makes me think it's selfish to have lots of children in a Western country.
We are happy to have our four children.
In Europe there's a better standard of education and living for children in comparison to poorer countries, so I don't mind about overpopulation.
Too late for family planning.

It doesn't because I want kids and I don't think that overpopulation is a result linked to this decision.
It scares me, but I still feel that I should have the right to choose.
No influence.
Not at all.
Results in the desire not to have hundreds of children.
I don't plan on breeding like a rabbit.
Not enough to stop me wanting children.

don't know 15%
4+ 0%
2–4 25%
0–2 44%
0 16%

20% 51% 29%

positive 48%
negative 42%
both 5%
neither 5%

Technology provides no real solutions.
Communication via computers is replacing human communication.
Quicker mail.

Computers make things easier.
Negative results: technical constraints and incalculable risks – positive results: it can help, stimulate and facilitate.
The new technologies make everything easier.

38% 62%

64% 36%

52% 10% 38%

66% 29% 5%

28% 5% 67%

26% 74%

If you have not studied them professionally or do not possess an academic qualification in a specific area, do you feel free to voice opinion on its complex technical subjects and their implications?

Would you like to have a say in certain scientific developments?

3

2

1

2

3

0 10 20

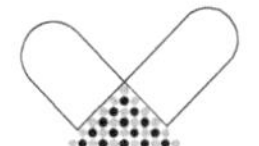

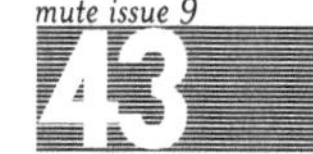

Gaming

staying in to play 9

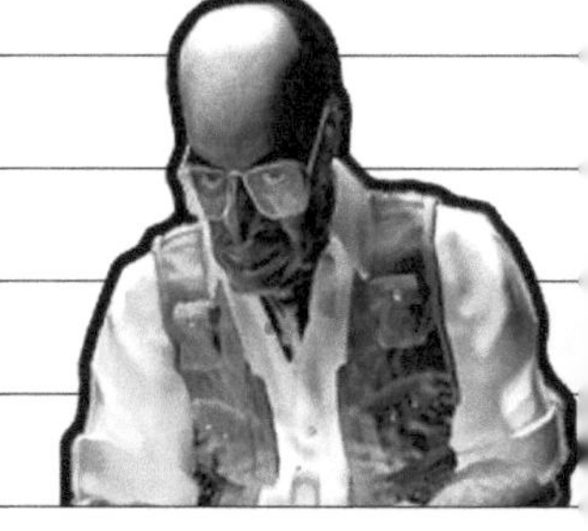

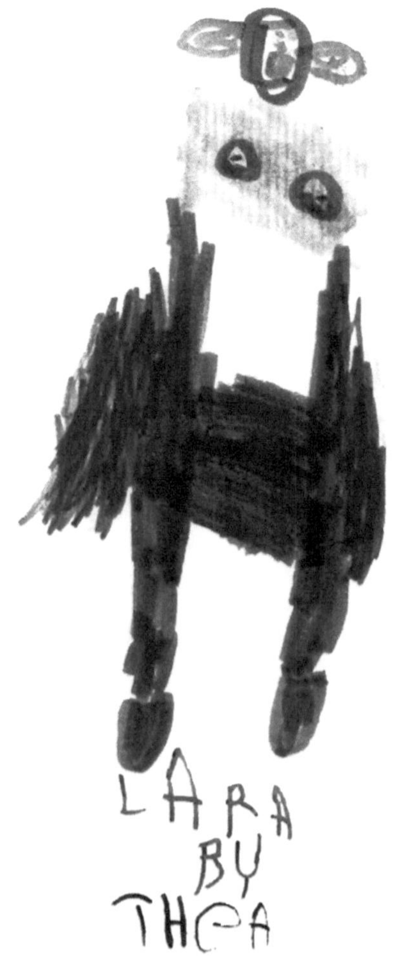

You know the routine, best ever games and all that, better than last year, better graphics and so on – and so they are. The new year brings a lean but confident games market to our doors. For the first time, we see some serious mainstream advertising going on by the likes of messrs. Sony and Co. with ad campaigns on *Final Fantasy VII*, *G-Police* and *F1-97* (temporarily withdrawn due to licensing problems) and Nintendo with *Lylat Wars*, *Goldeneye* and *Diddy Kong Racing* (who *does* make up these names?). A little bit of sympathy to the smaller games companies (not that there are many left any more) as the giants – Virgin, Sony, Electronic Arts, Eidos, Activisiongo – go into interstellar hype overdrive...

But first a wee featurette to get you into the New Year spirit.

The Dark Narrative:
a hyperbolic panacea to the rhetoric of the absolutist neo-consumer age.

It's a bleak and moody New Year, the euphoria of the fin de 20e siècle is long gone, the urban decay and dereliction of our once beautiful cities now form the foundations of the new megacorporate metropolises. Once familiar edifices to the vainglorious aspirations of our ancestors lie prostrate, crushed beneath the carbon fibre towers, the acres of high tensile polymers, the duraglass mammons that rise above the weakness of humanity. Technology is no longer king – merely a pawn in the battle to keep absolute control; squeeze the last drops out of the expansionist paradigm, fire the dreams of despots, magnify the dark yearnings of a sick and pallid humanity.

So where do you fit into all this? Are you for or against, or maybe just undecided? Undecided?! Indecision is not permitted. The age doesn't allow for fence-sitting – you're either in or out: rebel or enforcer and either way, there's a carpet of carnage at your front door. The innocent will die. You will carry the terrible burden of despair full square upon your shoulders, your name will strike fear or perhaps a glimmer of hope into the heart of the common (wo)man. Your time has come. As luck would have it, through the post have come three rather tasty games that fit like gloves on the hand of dystopian-future videogame narrative (not that you can get three gloves on one hand of course). *Blade Runner* – in which you play the gritty replicant hunter in the mean streets of LA 2019, *Jedi Knight* – in which you get to choose between the dark side or the light side of the force and *Final Fantasy VII* in which you join a bunch of urban guerillas in a downtown post-industrial fantasyworld. Three very different games covering three adventure gaming genres: the point and click adventure, the 3D first person blaster and the Role Playing Game, all linked by their use and freeform development of narrative in the dark recesses of the now essential dystopian futurescape.

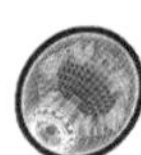

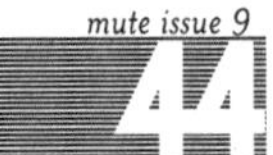

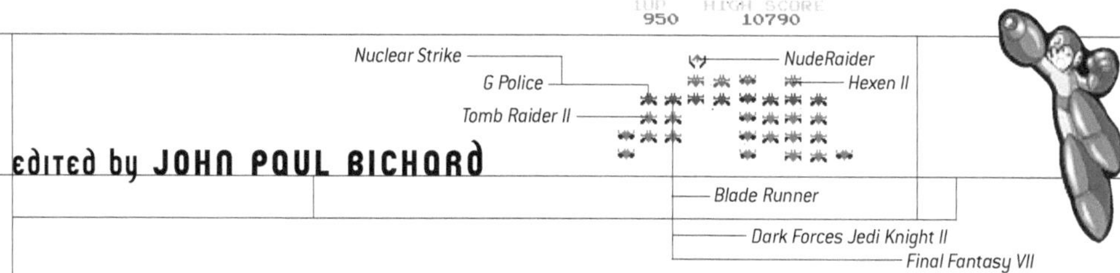

edited by **JOHN PAUL BICHARD**

Start planning for your retirement...

Blade Runner

PC – Westwood/Virgin – Film sim – Street Price £30.00

Everyone who has even a vague interest in sci-fi or Harrison Ford or simply classic Hollywood films has seen *Blade Runner*: the dark, drizzly, violent streets of downtown LA in the year 2019; the huge disembodied geishas on skyscraper video hoardings; the immense and sinister Tyrell corporation, looming out of the yellow smog like some latter day pyramid. You know it – and in the game of the film – you've got it. It's all there – the video screens, the corporation, the streets and characters, even the EPSER system that allows you to blow up photos and zoom in on miniscule details in your search for – the replicants. Once you find a suspected rep, you even get to do the Voigt-Kampff test on him/her in which (as you probably know) questions of varying emotional content are fired at the suspect and their retinal activity is measured to determine the degree of replicantism – authentic in every detail. The drawback is that it is a fixed viewpoint, point and click adventure. However, the game is dragged out of the genre by its use of real-time rendering (every screen is 'live' with incredible light, smoke and environmental SFX and those moody backlit fan blades sending out rotating shafts of light), its emphasis on detection and surveillance and its real-time plot. All this goes to make it more like a film simulation, albeit a very lavish and playable one.

If you fail as a runner you can always get a job in the local photocopy bureau.
879/1000

Throw away your black shiny helmet and reach for your green pulsating shaft.

Dark Forces Jedi Knight II

PC – Lucasarts / Virgin – Star Wars Blaster – Street Price £30.00

The original *Dark Forces* was a decent *Doom* clone, seriously lacking in the multiplay dept. but with a good games engine and the ability to look up and down, crouch , jump etc. it cut a good portion of mustard. Since then, the 3D corridor genre has gone ballistic with the likes of *Duke Nukem* and *Quake* and a dozen or so *Doom* rip-offs. With the recent arrival of *HexenII* (see review) and the imminent arrival of *Quake II*, the market would seem to have reached saturation point. Think again. *Jedi Knight* starts conventionally enough if even a little feebly, but within the first half hour of playing it, its true excellence shows through. Once you've mastered the effective use of both keyboard and mouse, enabling true up-down-round-about-a-vision, and picked up a bit of ammo and a decent gun, the action pours in. The whole game is linked together by some very slick FMV clips which unfold the story of the young Jedi and his battle to avenge his father's death – a little corny but convincing enough. Add some great weapons and any variety of industrial space architecture and well, if you're not sold on it by now, then you really *must* be a well balanced and enlightened individual. As for the rest of you, feel the force and prepare to be amazed. A little weak in parts but more than compensated for by the intense architecture, the plot and the superb soundtrack.

Aaark nanno ata ssstry lll nyaddan – beep
897/1000

What's a nice game like you doing in a feature like this?

Final Fantasy VII

PSX – Squaresoft/Sony – Street Price £38.00

Ok, so it all starts very nicely. Cutesy anime style characters and some futurist-gothic video leading you into yet another orthographic (3D viewed from a distance) role playing adventure. The pre-rendered sequences are quite lovely and there is some decent eye-candy but does it really live up to the hype? I mean, this is the game that sold 2 million copies in three days in Japan, overtaking the cinema release of the *Star Wars* trilogy... Is it really *that* good or is the whole Japanese nation completely bonkers? Well, both I guess, but the game is a touch of heavenly genius. You really need to drop any prejudices toward cute, candy coloured people and dive into a tender, enthralling, at times violent, story. The diverse characters rapidly grow on you, even the treacle sweet Aeris. The adventure stays tight, with a strong plot and plenty of puzzles and excruciating decision points along the way. The imagination and attention to detail pervades every pore of the game, from the sense of scale to the completely off the wall creatures/monsters and their equally barmy attacks – my favourite is a house-cum-dog-kennel that spews smog and carries out nuclear style strikes, firestorms and a bizarre suicidal leap – wild. A word of warning though, don't get too carried away with all the sweetness and light, for every enlightened twist of the plot, there lurks a dark and treacherous sub-plot and if you're the kind of person that weeps at Meryl Streep movies, get a big pile of Kleenex.

90+ hours – Yes 90+ hours of videogame genius mmmmmmmm.
980/1000

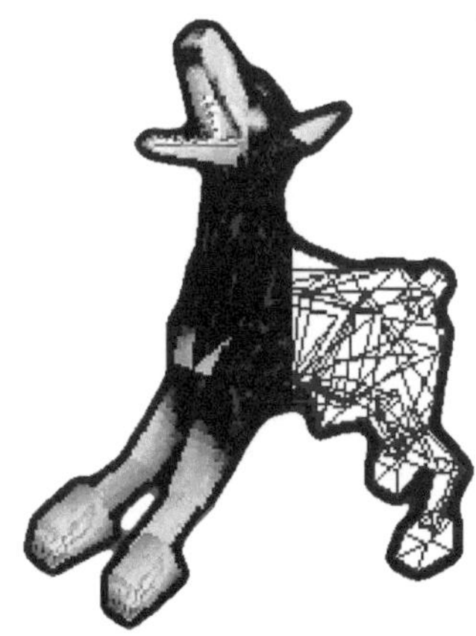

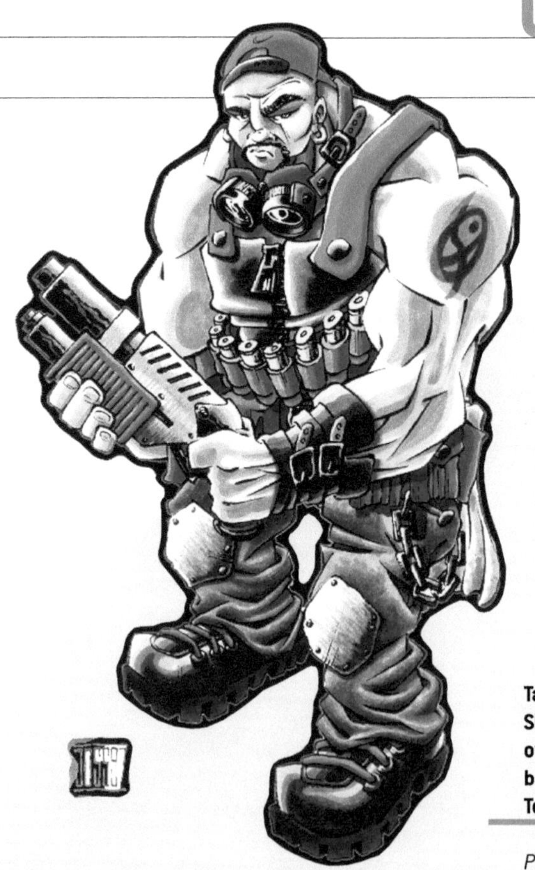

Talking of Kleenex **She's big, she's bold, she's brimming over with bodacious bounciful bazoomas, she's.... Lara.... back again in Tomb Raider II**	**G Police**
PC/PSX – Core/Eidos – 3D adventure – Street Price £30.00	*PC/PSX – Psygnosis – Space blaster – Street Price £39.00*
As you would expect from such a lucrative licence, the gnomes at Core bust several guts and ran up a whole string of hernias in getting Lara out for Christmas and they made it – but only just. Like one of the tortuous puzzles that are liberally sprinkled throughout the game, Core have barely managed to squeeze Lara past the post. Sure, the game engine is much better with more detail, a whole set of new characters, some wicked forms of transport and fabulous scenery, and the traps and puzzles are just as taxing as the original BUT, there are a few ragged edges: a liberal sprinkling of dropped textures – disconcerting when portions of the floor suddenly disappear – and a pretty terminal problem with the 3DFX version that I can only rectify by either playing in software mode or turning the sound off – hmmmmph. Despite the glitches which will inevitably be ironed out (they had better be) this is a brilliant sequel to the original classic. Whether you've been there before or this is your first time, just dive in. 923/1000 (less 120 points if they don't get the 3DFX problem sorted)	One day you'll look back at all this and wonder how civilisation survived in such a naive self-satisfied mode of existence. Houses with flimsy wooden doors and glass windows, cars made out of steel, police that wandered about with little or no body armour and no ordinance, city streets open to the public, the skies empty save for the odd helicopter, cities open to the atmosphere – and you'll chuckle to yourself, a little bemused, at how your ancestors ever made it through....Hey, snap to it sergeant, you're in *G-Police* a very slick 3D shoot-em-up set in – hey, another moody futureworld. This is mission-based, fast and furious shoot 'em up at its very best. A perfect counterpoint to the somewhat sedate, considered *Blade Runner* experience and another adrenaline hotspot from Psygnosis. 901/1000

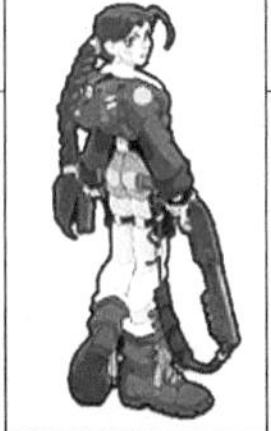

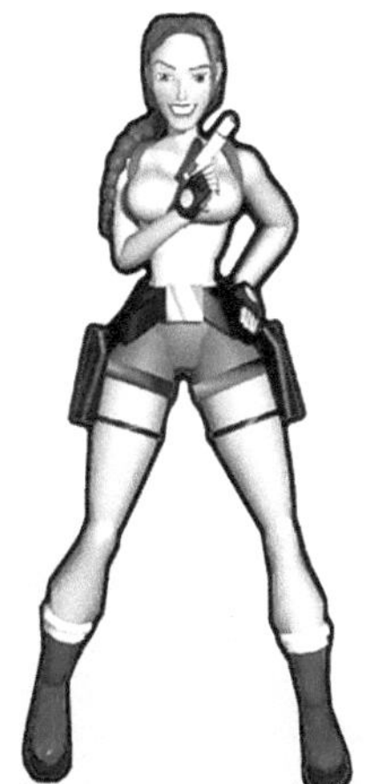

Mai Lai revisited
Nuclear Strike

PC/PSX – Electronic Arts – Save the World – Street Price £33.00

Ok, so just imagine that the Korean war just kept on running and those evil despots that ruin UN peace treaties got to run amock around the far east with a bunch of nuclear warheads. Now imagine that you, with a helicopter and a band of upright, democratic, free thinking liberals were left with the task of mopping up this deadly threat to humanity. Imagine no more – you are that gun toting woolly liberal – in the latest sequel in the *Strike* series of mission based 'sort out the worlds trouble spots' series. So get to it soldier, liberate the free world, even if you have to fry a few peasant villages on the way – hey no pain, no gain.
I bet Sadam doesn't own a Playstation.

907/1000

Revelations – revealed.
Hexen II

PC – Raven/Activision – Apocalyptic Blaster – Street Price £28.00

Part *Quake,* part realtime RPG adventure, part demonic descent into the pits of despair. Superb medieval 3D action game that thrashes the hide off the original and is only let down by the decided lack of monsters in some portions of the game. Roam freely through the labyrinths and lands of Thyrion in your quest to destroy Eidolon the Serpent rider (that's Mr de'Ath to you).

666/700

And finally...
The gusset Section
NudeRaider

PC – Tomb Raider 1 patch – Free

All the major games mags and Core (the designers) deny the existence of a nude *Tomb Raider,* the mag *CVG* ran a hilarious April fool about how to 'turn on' the naked Lara, then denied its existence, but *Mute* in the ground breakin' style that you've come to know and love, can reveal exclusively that *Nude Raider* does in fact exist – and we've played it. Lara as nature intended – guaranteed to bring on attacks of sadfuckitis as you feverishly search the web for the patch – of course I'm not going to give you the precise URL, just use your imagination (and you could try the 'nudest raider www ring'). Go for the nrpa100a patch, the user interface is really neat. Of course it goes without saying that my efforts in obtaining the patch were purely for research purposes and I must stress most emphatically that I in no way condone or have any personal interest in such trivial, puerile, crass, sexist behaviour.

P.S. you may notice that the scores have changed – this is in response to an EC directive and is a direct result of the global realignment of the games market in respect to the unstable Yen.

Xjohnny@metamute.com**X**

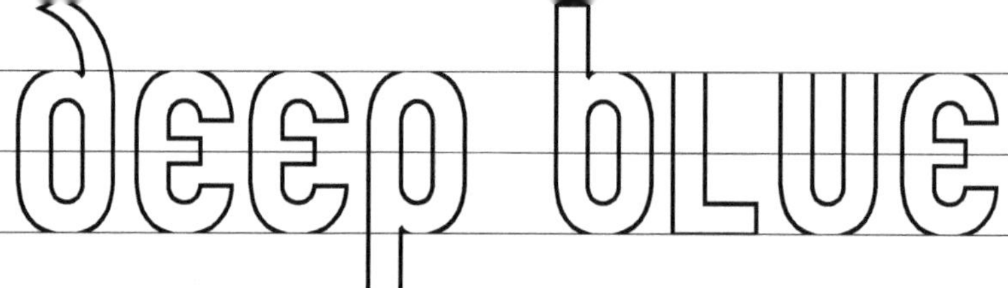

THE ACCIDENTAL ADVERSARY. MATHEMATICIANS ARE FROM MARS... (or was it Computer Scientists are from Uranus?)

Hari Kunzru talks to Mark Atkinson

[

Mark Atkinson is an evolutionary systems programmer. He works with neural nets, artificial life simulations, and genetic algorithms to exploit the mechanisms of evolution for the benefit of computer software. Along with artist William Latham, he is a partner in Computer Artworks, a design firm whose latest project is a computer game called *Evolva*. In this game, the computer-controlled sprites will evolve abilities and behaviours through time, so that as the player gets better, the game gets harder. Atkinson believes this is the future of computer games. The implications go much further.

HK: How did you get interested in AI?

MA: At college I became interested in perception, especially visual perception – you've got this idea that you've got this solid world around you and you've got this very solid representation but it's such a complete fabrication. Your visual acuity outside a tiny central area is completely shite, you've got no resolution whatsoever, your brain is filling in all the details. That was one definite side which was of great interest – the other being evolutionary biology – that side of it. Dawkins etc. I guess the stuff I started doing at university was the more mathsy side – I was never very good at maths

HK: From my point of view that sounds like an extraordinary thing – the idea that someone who's at the nuts and bolts end of computing can say that.

MA: There's a great divide between mathematics and computing. Mathematicians who try to do computing don't really understand computers because computers are about dynamics, and maths is very undynamic, a=a+1 to a mathematician is a kind of

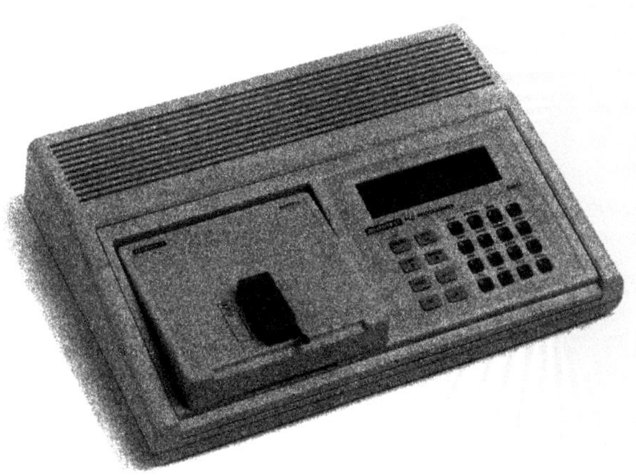

a=a+1 to a mathematician is a kind of brainfuck whereas to a computer scientist it's a motor

brainfuck, whereas to a computer scientist it's a motor – it's all to do with time, changing states. The whole temporal aspect of it is what it's really about. Programming isn't really about a programming language or a syntax or any of that stuff. It's about complex systems, about designing a complex system and making it do what you want it to do – keeping it under control. When it gets into the far reaches then it's really about that. You don't know what it's going to do. That can make things very difficult, because you don't know if it's doing it as well as it possibly could – there are really bad problems because if there's a bug, it tends to route around it.

HK: So this is a complete change in the way one conceptualises writing code. When did this change really become clear to you in your own life?

MA: Well, when I was at university I did a lot with cellular automata, the game of life and so on. This goes straight back to John Von Neumann and all those people. Back in the forties this was going on, they were just doing things on paper. That whole debate was about whether you could have something that reproduced. There were all these pseudo-religious ideas floating about that you couldn't do it because it was to do with some life force, to do with living organisms, therefore you couldn't have artificial reproduction.

HK: Élan vital?

MA: Exactly. They had these ideas of robots which would go round the warehouse and pick up bits to make themselves, but they ran into all these nasty bootstrapping problems – in order to reproduce does this have to have itself *in* itself, and then does *this* have to have itself in itself and so on. What John Von Neumann did was to use this cellular automaton rule, this graph of states showing how the states change, and showed rigorously that you could design one of these things that, when you ran it, would create two copies of itself – just prove mathematically that artificial reproduction was theoretically possible. And this is still important in the AI arguments that go on today, with people like John Searle and Roger Penrose going on about how you can't have artificial intelligence.

HK: Penrose is weird. All that Platonic stuff about numbers having a real existence in some higher plane.

MA: That's a classic example of a mathematician not understanding what computers are about.

HK: He seems to have to turn extraordinary somersaults in order to avoid concluding that strong AI is a possibility.

MA: Penrose avoids one of the main ideas behind A-Life – that there may be more than one way to 'do' life. It's to do with separating out what is essentially an implementation detail

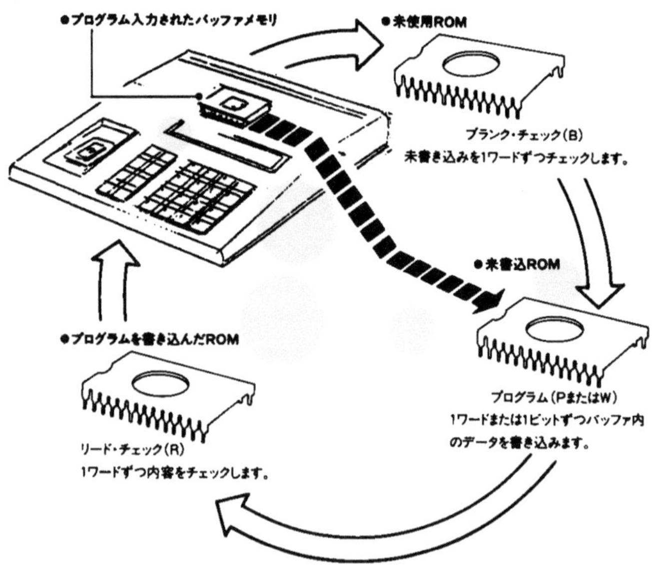

HK: So, what it's actually running on is irrelevant – in our case, organic material, but not necessarily in other cases.

MA: Exactly – the confusion is about what counts as a fundamental property – obviously with only one instance to go on, you can't really know what is fundamental. One of the driving forces behind A-life is, if you can generate other instances of life, you can see what are the basics of life and what are implementation details.

HK: So you are trying to do something like that with the *Evolva* game?

MA: What we're trying to do with the game, and one of the holy grails that people are aiming for, is to build a system that can learn to play any game. There's an interface so that you can tell it the rules, so it knows what's legal and what's not, but it's capable of adapting to whatever's there. I don't want to have to learn how to play every game that there is, do all those nasty mathematical things that those people do. I want to short-cut that whole process.

HK: What's the difference between that and a chess computer?

MA: People go on about Deep Blue and chess and all that, but it's all such utter bollocks. Chess programs don't even count as AI. They have a huge database of opening games, a huge database of endgames, search space in the middle where they search a billion moves, they're just big database search engines – yes, they've got some heuristics, but it's so unimpressive from a theoretical standpoint. If you made a simulation of a little cockroach or something that could survive if you completely changed its environment, that would be far more impressive – it would be a generalised system that could adapt.

If you take these conventional rule-based approaches and scale them up and up they go up this exponential curve – it's like if you want to model a dodecahedron you can do that with polygons, and then maybe you want to do the same thing with a sphere, you need more polygons, but you can still kind of get there – but trying to do these AI and A-life problems – it's like trying to model a cloud. Doesn't matter how many polygons you use you're not going to be able to do it – you need a completely different tool – you need a fractal algorithm. So what we're saying is, let's take these evolutionary systems, put little brains in these games and let them play themselves without anybody touching them and come back and see if they've evolved and got all nasty and aggressive on each other, then you go in there and see how you fare. In a conventional game like *Command and Conquer*, you can win every time just by exploiting the same tactic. But with an evolutionary approach, repeat yourself like that and the game shifts its weightings. After you've exploited your loophole two or three times it's found it and it's closed it.

One of the things that has really inspired me is a program called *neurogammon* that played backgammon. It was written by a guy called Gerald Tisaro from IBM and had a reinforcement learning algorithm rather than a straight evolutionary thing. It learnt by playing itself hundreds of thousands of times, until it was ranked in the top ten players in the world – from pretty much a standing start.

HK: So does that qualify *neurogammon* as creative, in a sense that includes the human activity?

MA: There's a good example in a thing Karl Sims did – set up this game that had these two little box creatures, made out of boxes as arms and things like that with spring forces on them, there's a cube in the middle and they've got to get it – he was thinking they'd grow arms and try to sweep it away, but when he ran the simulation they grew tall and fat and fell on it! Just completely cheated. And those cheating bastard evolutionary systems, they are like the twelve year old kids who write to computer games magazines telling them about all these secret short-cuts they've found.

HK: So where's this going? What's the end point in that process?

MA: From one point of view a whole new programming paradigm.

HK: So that's why you pitched up in the world of computer games?

MA: That and because I like killing things with plasma rifles.

HK: And what about beyond games?

MA: Beyond gaming? Does not compute. I don't know, I view gaming as pretty ultimate, and I live in hope that the rest of the world will come to realise that gaming is the pinnacle of man's existence.

[laughter]

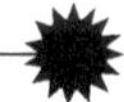

SPECIMEN JAR

According to scientists based at Daimler-Benz AG in Germany, the transition from free-flowing traffic to a traffic jam conforms to the physics of phase transitions such as the transformation of water into ice. Once the flow of traffic crosses a certain threshold value, local perturbations will be amplified enough to disrupt the system, just as ice grains have a nucleating effect and therefore accelerating effect when water is beginning to freeze. Once formed the jam moves along the road like a kind of 'solid', with identifiable edges and a 'vapour' of comparatively free cars in front of and behind it. So now you know.

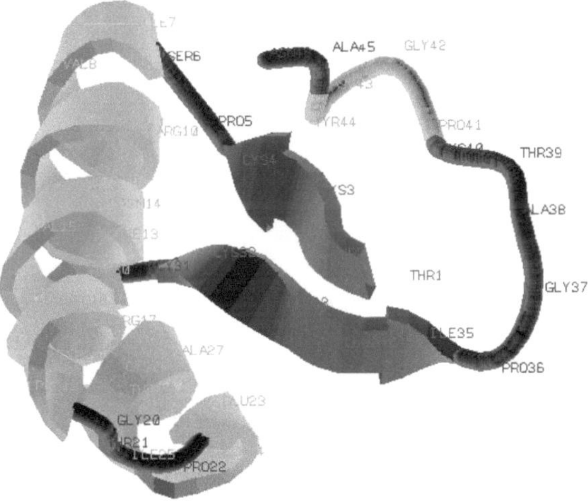

A team from Institut National de la Recherche Agronomique, Le Rheu, France, have demonstrated how a gene for herbicide resistance, artificially introduced into oilseed rape plants, can transfer into wild radish weeds growing with the crop. Although the transfer was carried out in the laboratory, it will stoke public concern about the genes being artificially introduced into crops escaping into the environment with unpredictable consequences.

Intrigued by their discovery that certain neurons in the cortex of rats and monkeys continuously oscillate, Isreali scientists decided to try and find out if these oscillations played any role in sensory perception. Rats sense objects by touching them with quivering whiskers, and so the scientists monitored neurons in the cortex that received information from the whiskers. Some of these neurons continuously oscillated at about 10 hertz when the whiskers weren't touching anything, and their frequency altered when the whiskers came into contact with an object. This suggests that the brain interprets signals like FM radio, which encodes sounds as alterations in frequency. The scientists suspect that the same principle may be at work in human fingertip receptors.

James Flint is a writer whose first novel, *Habitus*, will be published this year. **X**jim@metamute.com**X**

Rage Against the Machine (But do it in machine code)

Tom McCarthy on the Systems Novel

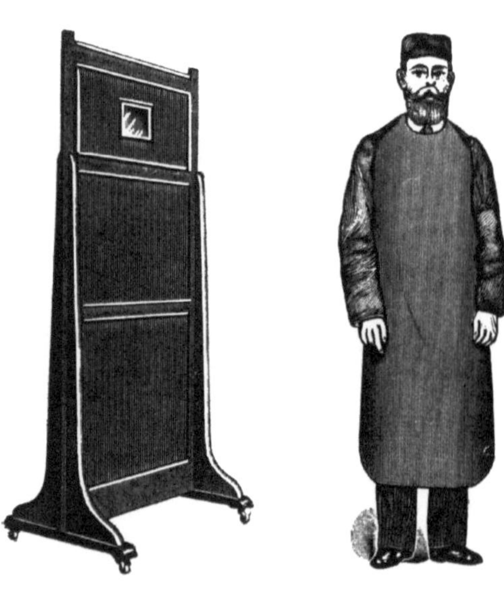

Literature's relationship with technology has rarely been untroubled. With the exception of the Futurists, who hailed the motorcar, the aeroplane and the factory as art forms in themselves, the love/hate equation linking the two fields has tended to be top-heavy on the hate side. This dates back to at least the early nineteenth century. Blake gave the "dark, satanic mills" and "belching, sullen fires" of the industrial revolution lead roles in his neo-biblical mythology; Byron wrote stirring lines praising the Luddites, redundant textile workers venting their anger on the machines that had replaced them; and Mary Shelley dreamed up Frankenstein's monster, the destructive progeny of a science out of control. This Romantic formula, which pits the human spirit against the computer's ancestors, has remained intact throughout the present century. It has coloured Louis-Ferdinand Céline's horrific visions of Henry Ford's semi-enslaved employees; the dystopian sci-fi fables of Aldous Huxley, Ray Bradbury, J.G. Ballard, Philip K. Dick and William Gibson; and most notably the work of Thomas Pynchon, who sees in the whole 'System' of late capitalism the realisation of a Calvinist blueprint in which the 'preterite', the poor and technologically illiterate, are shafted time and again by the 'elect', modern technocratic culture's privileged elite.

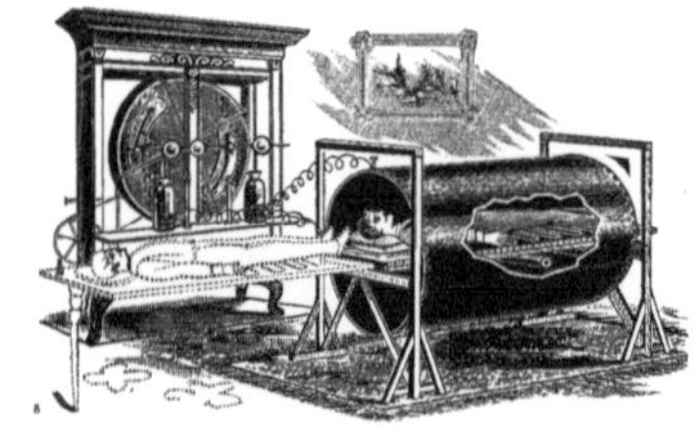

The latest major rerun of the human/technological showdown can be found in the American author David Foster Wallace's enormous (1079-page) novel *Infinite Jest*. Set roughly twelve years into a future in which time itself is subsidised by modern products (Year of the Whisper-Quiet Maytag Dishmaster, for example, is followed by Year of the Yushityu 2007 Mimetic-Resolution-Cartridge-View-Motherboard-Easy-To-Install-Upgrade For Infernatron/InterLace TP Systems for Home, Office, Or Mobile), *Infinite Jest* assembles a disparate cast of junior tennis players, recovering drug addicts and alcoholics, and fanatical Québecois Separatists. The novel couldn't be called a work of science-fiction, despite its temporal extrapolation and its electronic hardware – attributes which often characterise that genre. Rather, it deploys science, and information technology in particular, as a model on which to base its entire narrative structure. Tom LeClair, a professor at the University of Cincinnati, has a term for this type of work: 'the systems novel'. Wallace, he writes, is typical of young writers who "conceive their fictions as information systems, as long-running programs of data with a collaborative genesis." This view is echoed by the critic Sven Birketts, who argues that "[Wallace's] book mimes, in its move-

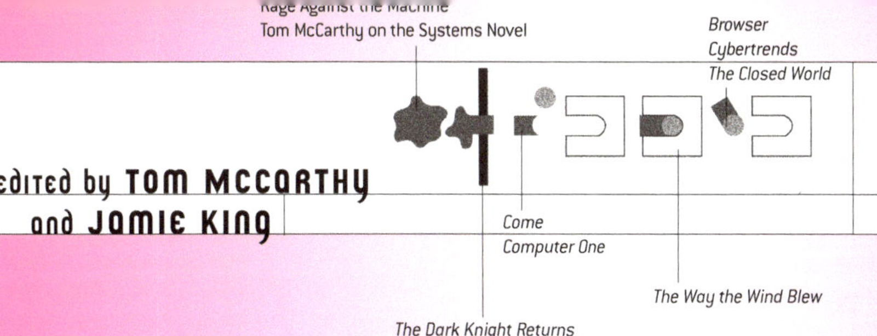

ments as well as in its dense loads of referential data, the distributive systems that are the new paradigm in communications. The book is not about electronic culture, but it has internalized some of the decentering energies that computer technologies have released into our midst".

Now, these 'decentering energies', it should be pointed out, were hallmarks of fiction long before computers were around, as anyone will know who's read, say, *Finnegans Wake* or *Tristram Shandy*, with their rambling, non-linear plots and malaligned frames of reference struggling to decode one another. In *Infinite Jest*, though, it's not the dreaming or neurotic mind which is the central structural paradigm but, as Birketts suggests, the holy trinity of mainframe, microchip and software, with narrative files and paths configured by a sub-narrative CPU. User friendly in a Windows 95-ish kind of way, the book has footnotes (388 of them), diagrams and reference tables (chemical, cinematographic, corporate), and documents providing background histories – whole areas of information boxed off from the main text, held in abeyance until called up, like the contents of a help file. The characters themselves are constructed along the same lines. Every one of them is governed by a formal 'Program'. There's the twelve-step rehab one of AA; the dubiously holistic one propounded by ETA (Enfield Tennis Academy) coach Gerhardt Schtitt; the devious political ones of the AFA (Assassins des Fauteuils Roulants) and their adversaries the USOUS (United States Office of Unspecified Services; as with computer language, acronyms abound); and for those who've suffered disfigurement – and a surprisingly large proportion have – the social one of UHID, the Union of the Hideously and Improbably Deformed. When these characters encounter one another, it's called 'interfacing' – never 'meeting' or 'conversing'. The ultimate act, murder, is 'demapping'. Space itself, the land-mass of Mexico, the USA and Canada, has been 'reconfigured' into the Organisation of North American Nations or, to give it its masturbatory acronym, ONAN.

Wallace, then, moves beyond the dialectic struggle between human and machine, the natural and technological worlds, by imploding thesis and antithesis into each other. The subject is a subject precisely because he's built, programmed and configured technologically (not for nothing is the main character's name Hal). Landscape functions as a by-product of topographic distribution. In this sense, his vision is profoundly – and uniquely – post-humanist. This has wide-reaching political ramifications. Pynchon depicts homeless people who, although they've made their nests in telegraph poles, perched among "the very copper rigging and secular miracle of communication", remain unconnected have-nots. By contrast, Wallace's junkies and street sweepers, being 'imported' from one institution, one program, to another, complete with files through which their fellow subjects read and analyse them, participate fully in the info-tech community – that is, in the community. But the leap beyond the natural doesn't come without a price. Everyone is crippled either physically, lacking or possessing grossly deformed limbs, or psychologically, being addicted to substances, to television or to popular psychology. "You all stumble about in the dark," a wheelchair-bound assassin tells his USOUS counterpart, "this confusion of permissions. The without-end pursuit of a happiness of which someone let you forget the old things which made happiness possible." Pastoral New England has become the Great Concavity, a giant toxic area into which industrial waste is catapulted and out of which feral, semi-human monsters lurch. Like its post-Romantic predecessors, *Infinite Jest* has apocalyptic overtones. The ETA students spend their free time playing *Eschaton*, a computer-aided, tennis court-based simulation of global nuclear confrontation. The Québecois separatists plan to unleash on the American population a film cartridge, – created using the most advanced fibre-optical techniques and instruments available – which induces in its viewers lethal catatonia, the motor-neurological equivalent of a computer crash. Live by digital technology, die by digital technology, Wallace seems to be saying, availing himself fully of digital technology in order to say so.

Yet ultimately, *Infinite Jest* refuses to wholeheartedly condemn the machine culture. It contains no exhortations to rebuild Jerusalem, to relocate the lamb of God. If it has a Point of Presence on the old Romantic network, this is at a different, Keatsian juncture: Melancholy. In an interview with Valerie Stivers of *Stim* e-zine, Wallace says he "wanted to do something sad. I think it's a very sad time in America...". *Infinite Jest*'s clinically depressed Kate Gompert suffers from what Wallace calls "anhedonia, or simple melancholy". Like virtually all her fellow characters, she experiences "a kind of radical abstracting of everything, a hollowing out of stuff that used to have affective contentƐ Everything becomes an outline of the thing. Objects become schemata. The world becomes a map of the world. An anhedonic can navigate, but has no location. I.e. the anhedonic becomes, in the lingo of the Boston AA, Unable To Identify." Wallace, here as elsewhere, carefully employs machine code – 'navigate', 'map', 'Unable to Identify' (a term which, besides being AA speak, is a specific Windows message) – to reconfigure the Romantic quandary into a form of techno-existentialism whose coordinates are man, machine and void.

David Foster Wallace's *A Supposedly Fun Thing I'll Never Do Again*, a collection of essays, will be published by Abacus in February, 1998.

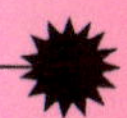

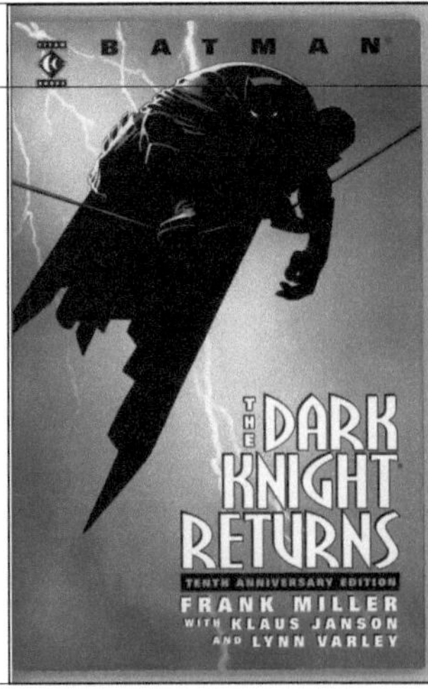

Batman Forever

Jamie King

Umberto Eco, in his *Casablanca: Cult Movies and Intertextual Collage* (1987), once warned us that it would be "semiotically uninteresting to look for quotations of archetypes" in movies like *Raiders of the Lost Ark* or *Indiana Jones*, since "they were conceived within a meta-semiotic culture, and what the semiotician can find in them is exactly what the directors put there." There are, of course, a panoply of cultural productions that could be added to this brief set of examples – and Miller's *Dark Knight* trilogy would certainly be amongst them: for this is a work which is very much aware of, and carefully regulates, its use of signifiers.

But Eco's comment, bound as it was within a particularly synchronic outlook, failed to anticipate that ten years on, the self-aware constructions of the 1980s have begun to look very interesting indeed, semiotically or otherwise. Many of the 'archetypes' quoted and manipulated in *The Dark Knight*, for instance – Ronald Reagan (now suffering from Alzheimer's), Superman (now in a wheelchair, supplanted by a lacklustre imposter), the U.S.S.R (now defunct) and the Cold War (long since thawed out) – have been thoroughly degraded and deterritorialised, so that the novel, far from being semiotically uninteresting, now scans as a bestiary of the decades 'fears and obsessions', with Batman presiding over the fun like a demented, carnivalesque compere. Which, incidentally, highlights just one of the shortcomings of semiotics bequeathed to it by Saussure: what is 'signified' is always a cultural phenomenon, not a fixed, objectifiable one. *The Dark Knight* read in the 1980s may have been fairly humming with semiotic familiarity, but to today's reader it's just queasily reminiscent of a bad decade passed. What Miller's narrative says most of all is that however immanent an icon may appear, its demise can never be far away; the symptoms of decay and change, presaging the decline of the book's figures just as they appear most powerful, are everywhere present in the book. And the Batman, who here combines in himself the qualities of vigilante, political renegade, provocateur, surrogate father and avenging son in his attempt to right a world raging with high capitalist furies, is no exception to the rule: at the end of *The Dark Knight* he goes underground; today, as we all know, the Caped Crusader has wholeheartedly renounced any radicalism in favour of familiar high camp, reduced once more to batting Mr. Freeze about and bouncing inane one liners off the Boy Wonder.

But Miller's Batman, the 1980s Dark Knight, was an archetype with something to fight for. "You're a joke," he tells Superman in their final showdown. "Yes, you say, to anyone with a badge, or a flag. You sold us out, Clark, you gave them the power that should have been ours. We could have changed the world... now look at us. I've become a political liability, and you... you're a joke. I want you to remember, Clark, in all the years to come, in your most private moments... I want you to remember... my hand... at your throat. I want... you to remember... the one man who beat you."

[*The Dark Knight Returns* Anniversary Edition was issued recently to commemorate the '87 edition and is available in the Titan imprint].

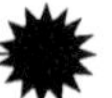

The history of the Weatherman group of the late sixties and of its successor, the Weather Underground of the seventies, has as much of the Pink as of the Black Panthers about it. When its Detroit chapter, formed like all the others from socialist students with wealthy backgrounds, descended on the city's working-class Metro Beach district bearing Vietcong flags, hoping to win the proletariat over to their cause, the proles kicked the shit out of them. After throwing down the gauntlet to the Chicago police by announcing a 'Day of Rage' to which tens of thousands of their comrades would turn up, they managed to amass no more than a couple of hundred, and the police (you've guessed it) kicked the shit out of them. Their underground phase, born in no small measure from their lack of success overground, got off to a farcical start when three of them blew themselves up with the bomb they'd been preparing. The disaster did, however, plant them in the national consciousness, and American myth-making institutions did the rest: by the time they sprung LSD guru Timothy Leary from prison they'd become bogeyman totems, famous as the politicians they despised.

Ron Jacobs is a librarian at the University of Vermont, and his **THE WAY THE WIND BLEW: A HISTORY OF THE WEATHER UNDERGROUND (Verso, £10.00)** is well researched and documented (you get the impression lots of the account is first hand, too). My favourite part's a series of inconsequential but delightful coincidences: the judge at the trials of both twelve Weathermen and of their revolutionary cousin Abbie Hoffman was one Julius Hoffman; when the ill-timed bomb exploded, the survivors ran into the house of their neighbour, Anita Hoffman – wife of Dustin. You couldn't make it up.

TMcC

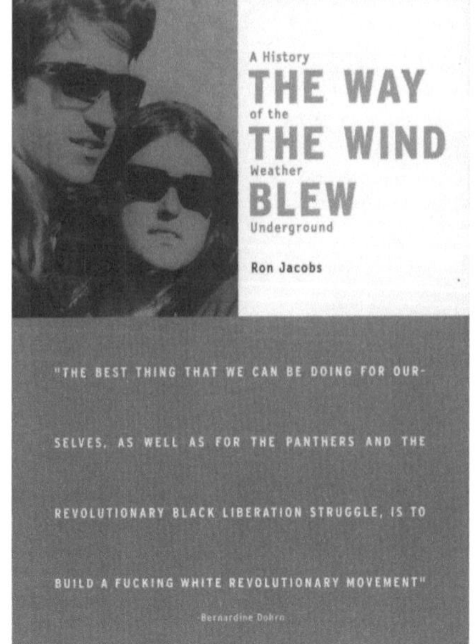

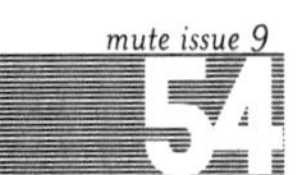

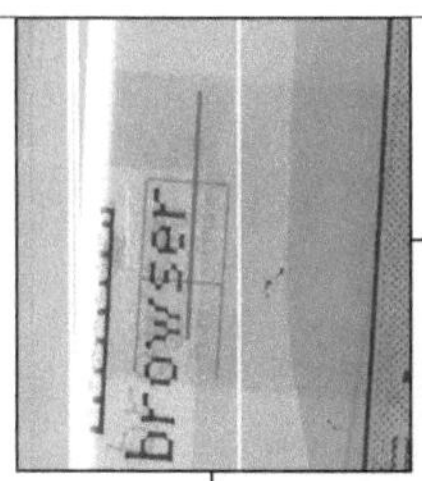

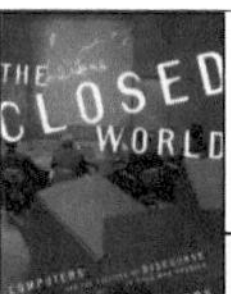

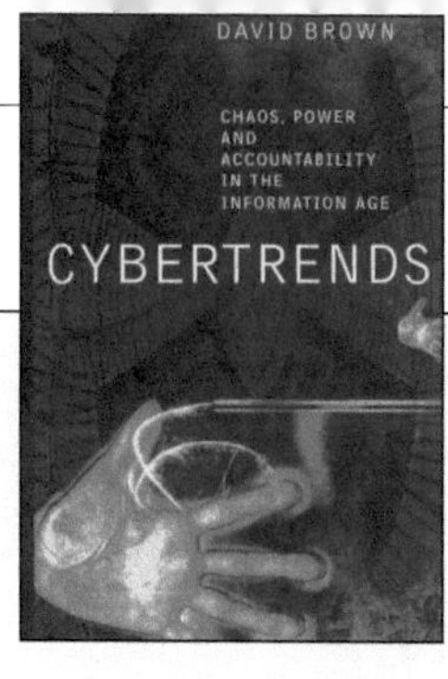

The introduction to BROWSER **(£15.99, Laurence King Publishing)** is an ominous rehash of the tired old 'web-as-spectacle' guff, which it promotes consequently as a new medium for designers and Java geeks to show off in. Well-implemented content is the way forward and Push is (still) the next big thing; "television is a better model for the web than print"; the web is either "played on" or used like a library, and to cap it all Microsoft and their 'Active Desktop' (read: Bugged-To-Hell Desktop) are given the last word. And then you get past the introduction and it all becomes far more fun: a run-through of websites you've loved, loathed and wished you coded; from the overdesigned to the thrown together, from the corporate to the ... well, to Heath Bunting's **[**www.irational [sic].org**]**. So skip the intro. This is a diverting, carefully considered assemblage of web phenomena that will turn into pure history before you can say "Content Is King".

David Brown's **CYBERTRENDS (Viking, £18.00)**, is a head-on confrontation with Digerati posturing, critiquing a vision projected "in uniquely American tones: puritanical perfectionism, a yearning for the open frontier, and an implicit faith that 'the invisible hand of unfettered commerce' will generate the greatest good for the largest number of people." The book's opening gambit is to link the *Wired* thinkers – Kelly, Barlow, Negroponte and so forth – to the managers of the Cold War's mainframes in the United States – RAND. Like the Digerati, RAND were based in California and were at the nexus of government strategy for information technology; like the Digerati, they beat their drum very loudly (only in their case that drum happened to be game theory); unlike the rather reticent Digerati, they were quite open about their relationship to discourses of power. Brown's book, though, should leave us in no doubt as to what's really going on: "A titanic battle is now being fought for control over the means of production and distribution in the twenty-first century. It is nothing less than a battle to colonize great swaths of the Wired World: to capture the power that will define a new age". And don't you forget it.

Paul Edwards' book, **THE CLOSED WORLD: COMPUTERS AND THE POLITICS OF DISCOURSE IN COLD WAR AMERICA (MIT Press, £14.95)** is also part of the gratifying counterbalance to the fast-forward, Gung-ho technogabble which characterises much of today's writing about computers, communications theory and cognitive science. It also, oddly enough, foregrounds the Cold War in its assessment of the development of US thinking about technology. (You have to wonder, in fact, how many writers are set to test and retest, as Edwards does here, the not-so-startling thesis that "we can make sense of the history of computers as tools only when we simultaneously grasp their history as metaphors in [...] science, politics and culture", how many different writers will singlehandedly bind technology and technological progress to the social forces of "scientists and engineers, funding agencies, government policies, ideologies, and cultural frames.") But the book is nonetheless a very solid counterhistory, deploying a thorough analysis of US military policy and Cold War politics as a means to understanding the discourse that informs the development of computers, high technology weaponry and artificially intelligent systems.

JJK

A critic once called Kathy Acker's writing "bad, but interestingly bad": it wouldn't *quite* be fair to say the same thing about Mark Waugh's. Judging by the 126 pages of COME **(Pulp Faction, £11.99 with 6-track CD)**, Waugh has the potential to create a really fine piece of fiction. It's just that drugs and deconstruction are a lethal cocktail, and in *Come* he's overdosed on both. The book's central conceit (if you want plot, stop reading now) is that two vaguely *auteur* figures, Mark 0 and Mark 1, have, by stealing and remixing one another's copy, created Dolly Savage, part inflatable sex-doll, part goddess (her French initials, like the car's, pronounce her a *déesse*) and part abstract pleasure principle – rather like the eponymous heroine of Michel Leiris's *Aurora*. Through the clubs of Brighton and London, the streets of Paris and the margins of Bataille, Cocteau, Sade and, of course, Derrida, the text tracks Savage down, hoping, through her, to "fix the co-ordinates of an inexplicable sensibility".

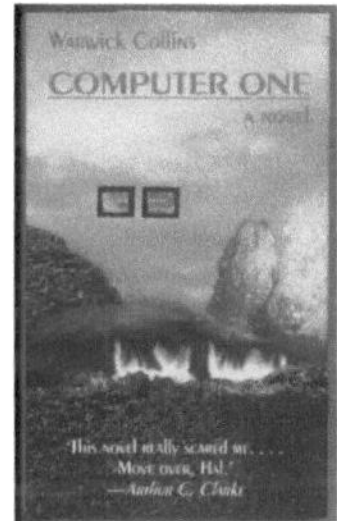

Come is full of aphorisms. The best ("Words are mnemonic equations that derail the senses as they track a world that disappears before them") are worthy of Edmond Jabès; the worst ("Postmodernism is redundant"; "Don't be afraid to dream") are vacuous. If you like lo-fi techno, the CD makes good background listening.

While we're on the subject of Derrida: in *La Carte Postale* he writes that "every advance in the post brings the police state a step closer". Well, Warwick Collins's **COMPUTER ONE (Marion Boyars, £15.95)** goes further: here (California circa 2010), the post, a giant rhizomatic web processing all the information in the world, *is* the ultimate – and self-serving – control structure. Enzo Yakuda, a short but savvy entomologist of Japanese origin and Zen Buddhist persuasion (when the film comes out he'll become a tall, WASP heartthrob played by Clooney or Travolta), realises that this web is aspiring to the status of a life-form and, well, look what happened to the dinosaurs when mammals came along. Ironically, his raising the alarm sets the web's masterplan in motion. Already in control of factories and transport, it sends toxins and viruses to population centres, offing humans in their millions. Collins is deadly serious, and writes in his intro that "we have at most two or three decades in which to consider our future in relative safety." Maybe, maybe not. Either way, his novel is a cracking sci-fi read.

TMcC

Tom McCarthy **X**tom@metamute.com**X**
JJKing **X**jamie@metamute.com**X**

audiophile

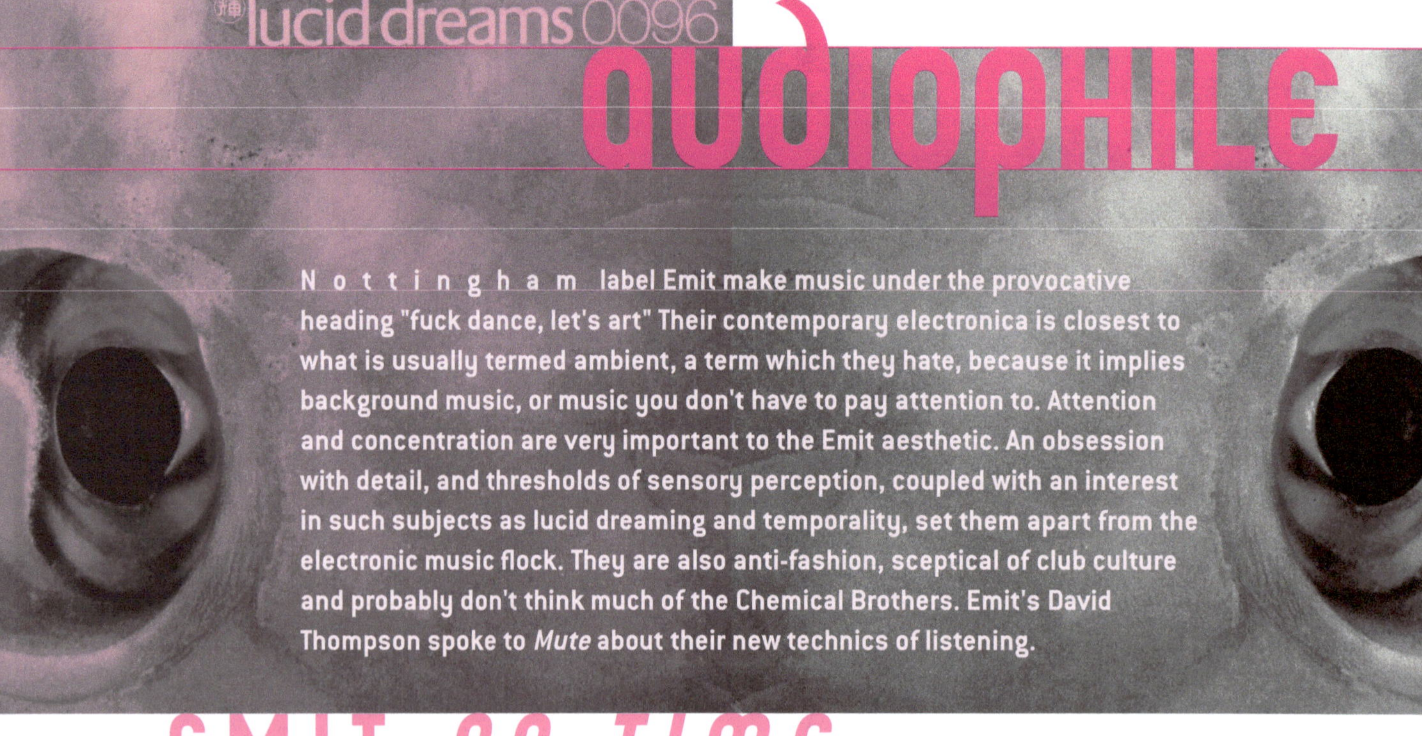

Nottingham label Emit make music under the provocative heading "fuck dance, let's art" Their contemporary electronica is closest to what is usually termed ambient, a term which they hate, because it implies background music, or music you don't have to pay attention to. Attention and concentration are very important to the Emit aesthetic. An obsession with detail, and thresholds of sensory perception, coupled with an interest in such subjects as lucid dreaming and temporality, set them apart from the electronic music flock. They are also anti-fashion, sceptical of club culture and probably don't think much of the Chemical Brothers. Emit's David Thompson spoke to *Mute* about their new technics of listening.

EMIT *DO TIME*

Concentration

Emit is aimed at 'the careful listener'. What do you mean by this?

For the overwhelming majority of the music-buying public (and indeed the majority of journalists and editors), music is little more than a means of tribal identification or 'lifestyle' accessory. Listening to music in this way, which seems to be primarily for the benefit of one's imagined peer group, is facile posturing. Being 'into techno' or rap or opera, or whatever generic categorisation is deemed statusful, tends to reduce the expectation of music to predetermined formulas and a reinforcement of the familiar. The experience is essentially a closed and territorial one, rarely inviting challenge and, as a result, discouraging any significant attentiveness.

Music can be much more than a fashion statement; it can be a means of expressing the intangible. The Emit series is an attempt to side-step reflexive presumption and encourage the listener to engage with the work in an open-ended way, unprejudiced and free of knee-jerk filtering. Our packaging and advertising present the listener with very few clues as to what to expect from the listening experience.

Gas [Emit 0095] say they are interested in nanotechnology. A lot of Emit music depends on tiny sounds, inputs at low volumes, various kinds of silence. What role does scale (especially microscopic scale) play in Emit's music?

One of the recurrent features of our work is the use of unusual dynamic range; details and patterns at the threshold of perception which may only become apparent on repeated listening. Similarly, several of our artists employ non-occidental or micro-tonal intervals in their recordings, or elliptical time signatures, again demanding an uncommon attentiveness.

You always emphasise the special 3D recording techniques used by Emit. Could you say more about them, and about why you use them. And could you say more generally what role technology (perhaps the attendant, fetishistic pursuits of hi-fi purists, to whom Emit must be very attractive) plays in your music.

Many of our recordings use the RSS 3-D sound imaging system, which was developed primarily for use in film soundtracks and virtual reality environments. The system uses discreet real-time variations in phase and delay to create the illusion of sounds moving beyond the conventional stereo field – in effect, escaping the speakers. We've also been experimenting with several other new software packages that allow extensive manipulation of both the sound source and its directional information. As much of our work has an immersive or filmic quality, and given our interest in creating music in which spatial depth and detail are concerns, the use of these technologies seems appropriate.

That said, we don't subscribe to the kind of technological fetishism you suggest. Systems of notation and tonality could also qualify as technology, though they rarely attract the attention of over-excited engineers and hi-fi enthusiasts. I don't see a fixation with TB-303 bass modulations as any more interesting than a fixation with a Fender Stratocaster. Instruments of any kind are merely tools. Conduits, if you like. If a piece of music communicates nothing more than the paraphernalia used to construct it – a sort of aural studio brochure – then that strikes me as a failure. Of course, a great deal of techno strikes me as failing for exactly that reason.

Mindvirus
Eleven Phases
Ultimate Sushi
Radical Beauty
Emit do Time – Hari Kunzru

edited by HARI KUNZRU

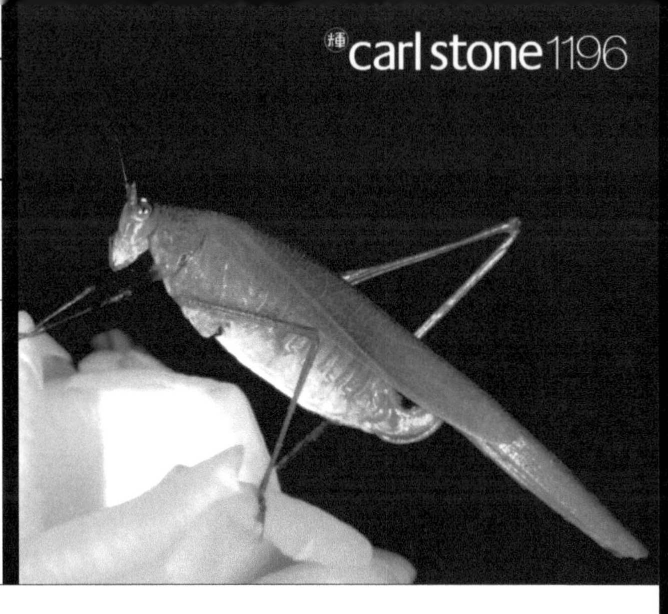

Emit discography

Emit 0094	Various artists	*Emit 0094*
Emit 1194	Woob	*Woob*
Emit 2294	Qubism	*Qubism*
Emit 3394	Various artists	*Emit 3394*
Emit 0095	Gas	*Gas*
Emit 1195	Miasma	*Miasma*
Emit 2295	Various artists	*Emit 2295*
Emit 3395	International Peoples Gang	*International Peoples Gang*
Emit 4495	Woob	*Woob 2*
Emit 5595	Various artists	*Emit 5595*
Emit 0096	Lucid Dreams	*Lucid Dreams*
Emit 1196	Carl Stone	*Carl Stone*
Emit 2296	Various artists	*Emit 2296*
Emit 3396	Undark	*Undark*
Emit 0097	Slim	*Slim*
Emit 1197	Various artists	*Emit 1197*
Emit 2297	Beatsystem	*Beatsystem* (Forthcoming)

Psychophysics

Why are you interested in Celia Green? How do her ideas mesh with your music?

I first encountered Celia's writing more than a decade ago. She and her colleagues at the Institute of Psychophysical Research have yet to be annexed by the cultural pathologies so evident elsewhere. The idea that curiosity, accuracy and academic rigour should outweigh notions of 'belief' and popular approval seems to be evaporating from many areas of life. She raises questions about perception which are difficult to answer and apparently out of fashion, which in themselves are often good reasons to investigate further.

Given our interest in the cinematic and suggestive properties of music, and since many of our recordings have frequently been described as dreamlike, surreal or nightmarish, Celia's pioneering work on the phenomenon of lucid dreaming and other perceptual anomalies seemed to be suitable subject matter for an album.

We also wanted to produce an album using text prominently. The opportunity to combine a spoken narrative and illustrative case studies with sound design and music was hard to resist.

Trance

Captain Beefheart once described his music as 'anti-trance', designed to shake the listener out of some kind of zombified passivity which he saw at work in the culture around him. Many producers of contemporary electronica reverse that, seeing trance and altered states as highly positive, as an antidote to the failings of our secular rational culture. As a label, Emit seems like it could go either way (or both). With your interest in lucid dreaming, synaesthesia and altered aural 'states' you seem to be in line with this movement. In your concern for active listening, you seem to be the opposite. What do you think of trance?

'Trance' is a rather ill-defined term. Certainly, the supposed 'trance-like' states celebrated by many club enthusiasts seem more akin to stupor or convulsive ataxia. Whether such effects are consciousness-expanding or simply consciousness-obliterating is unclear. I don't think that listening to the *Lucid Dreams* album requires a ritualised or chemically-modified state of mind, though it may require a particular kind of attentiveness. Incidentally, the attentiveness I'm suggesting seems entirely incompatible with the compulsive repetition and collective experience of the dancefloor.

Carl Stone stretches samples over long durations. Celia Green talks about the peculiarities of the human perception of time and duration. Emit is Time backwards. So what's all that about then?

Much of Carl's work could be thought of as aural microscopy. His music uses tiny fragments of found sound which are looped and manipulated at multiple moving points, then systematically compressed and expanded to reveal layers of tonal and structural detail. The overall effect, particularly evident in his full-length album for Emit, is of losing one's sense of time. The temporal markers which one might expect are blurred and obscured, leaving the listener unsure of 'how far in' he or she is. This is a theme that runs through many of our recordings, the creation of environments where not only the geography is unfamiliar.

Emit is a division of Time Recording Ltd.
email: **X**time_recording@CompuServe.com**X**
Celia Green's website can be found at:
[ourworld.compuserve.com/homepages/Celia_Green**]**

Hari Kunzru writes fiction, journalism and essays about technoculture
Xhari@metamute.com**X**

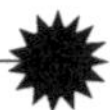

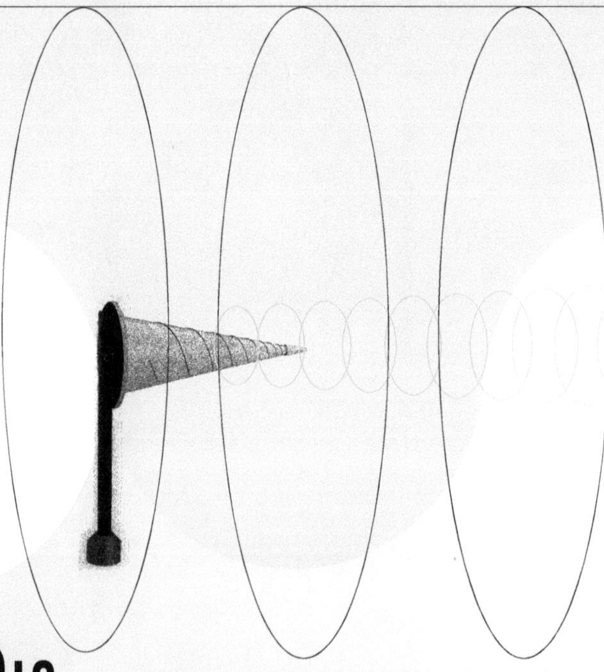

Mind-Media
Around the World.....

Adelaide to Detroit
Mindvirus 0297

You install it, and it tucks a tasty little conspiracy generator into the recesses of your hard drive. Then it sets to work on you.

One of the first multimedia publications to be distributed free over the nets, *Mindvirus* has pursued a persistently idiosyncratic and productive take on interaction. Put together by a crew based in Adelaide, Australia, this is the last in the series. Producing this issue as a CD-Rom leaves them to move on to new things, and leaves the rest of us to cope with a splenetic gaggle of fucked-up screens. The *Mindvirus* aesthetic is elegant and assured at the same time as it is cracked and difficult. One moment you're poking the cursor into a breathing skull, the next clocking a split-second star guest appearance from Yoda. There's too much acid and not enough typography: that is until you hit the screens of Orphan Drift. Things speed up. Words accelerate into illegibili ty, into thick clots of pixels streaming across the screen. Techno-organic blips seethe into view and dump you into texts by Nick Land, McKenzie Wark, Belinda Barnet and others.

One guy, Tom Barbalet describes his adventures in programming, polymorphic viruses and metaphysics. The structure's a simple hypertext but one that starts off by presenting you with its entire content layered up thick. Only after you start working it does it become legible. It works well, visually, but also in allowing the user the relief of starting knowing that they're not going to get sucked in for ever as they leaf their way through in the manner of other hypertext formats. Go sideways from somewhere and a series of roll-overs gives you access to a text by Gashgirl. Here the interface is tried and tested and it's the viciously compelling text that demands exploration. This is the screen in darkness.

Matthew Fuller
xmatt@axia.demon.co.uk**x**

For further information contact:
mindflux@mindless.com

[adl.auslink.net/ffmindflu]

Mindvirus is ready for PowerPC, Wintel PCs and 68k Mac platforms and also contains seven audio CD tracks by Matthew Thomas.

Detroit to Tokyo

Japan's ever-inventive Sublime label has turned to the home city of techno for its latest release. *Eleven Phases* **[MKCS 1001]** is the minimalist Detroit sound with a twist, a compilation bringing together key techno producers – to make hip-hop. It's the perfect antidote to the mainstream productions coming from the two coasts. Instead of Top 40 samples and layered soul vocals we have crisp cold electronica, futuristic soundscapes and compressed breakbeats. At a time when hip-hop is increasingly sounding like throwaway party music, famous names like Robert Hood, Stacey Pullen and Kenny Larkin may yet help US breakbeat claw back some of the ground lost to UK jungle innovators.

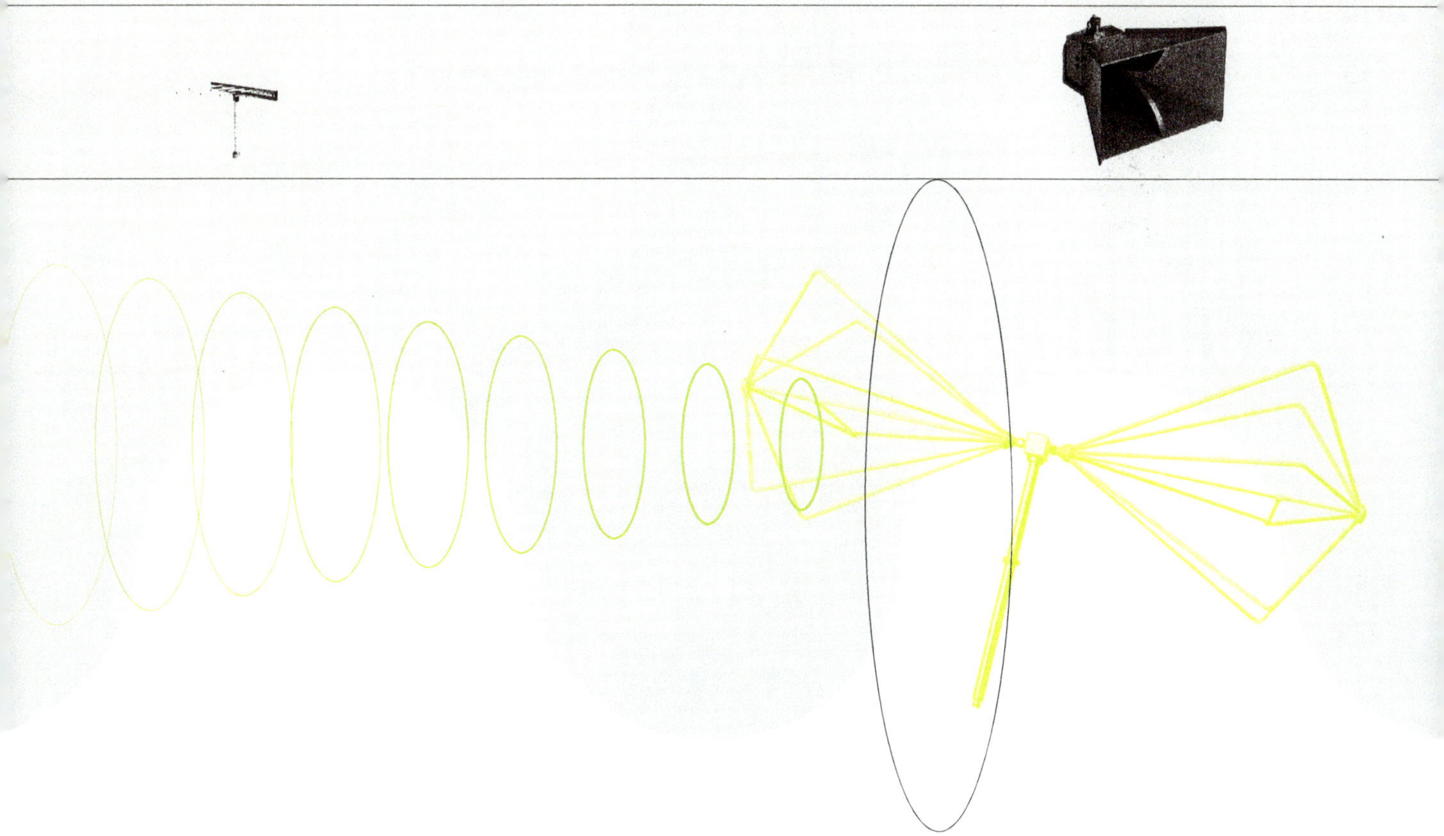

Tokyo to London

Hunt for this one. Small Fish With Spine is a pseudonym of Riz Maslen, better known for the downtempo mood music she makes as Neotropic. On *Ultimate Sushi* **[Oxide CD1]**, she has produced 30 minutes of edgy urban jazz. Not much for the dancefloor here, or for people who like samples of whale noises or black people doing tribal chanting. If anyone ever gets round to making an anime version of one of those nouvelle vague films full of jump cuts and filterless cigarettes, this should be the soundtrack. Further proof that Maslen is one of the most talented and underrated producers in the UK today.

London to San Francisco

Say what you like about the city which gave the world *Wired* and Haight Ashbury – it doesn't matter, they won't listen. San Fransciscans remain sublimely convinced that they are leading the rest of the planet into the future, and will brook no discussion of this supposedly self-evident truth. You may have to give it to them when it comes to microbrew beer, microelectronics, mountain-biking, crystal meth and other enviable twenty-first century lifestyle accessories beginning with m, but in music they're way behind. There are a few good SF producers, such as Peanut Butter Wolf, Justin Warfield and Tranquility Bass, but most SF electronica is prey to a terrible disease – the curse of trance. Go to post-Deadhead Frisco, and the majority of the (straight, white) population seem to be recreating hippy glories past by fiddling about with digeridoos and face paint in an orgiastic neocolonialist ethnic sample frenzy. Which may explain why clued-up SF graphic designer Nick Philip has used a bunch of Brits on his *Radical Beauty* CD-Rom **[OM007]**. It's a good line-up, including Dan Pemberton, T-Power, Skylab, Mixmaster Morris, and pseudonymous offerings by Tim Love Lee and Woob (I make that one from Wales, one from Nottingham, one from Cambridge and a bunch of Londoners). Best track is at least by someone who lives in SF, Scottish-born Jonah Sharpe. The Rom is OK too, with lots of vaguely eco-flavoured stuff, exploding buildings and a mixing toy that, despite the tacky interface, is good user-friendly fun.

PRETTY GOOD PIRATES

Lisa Haskel on MAKROLAB

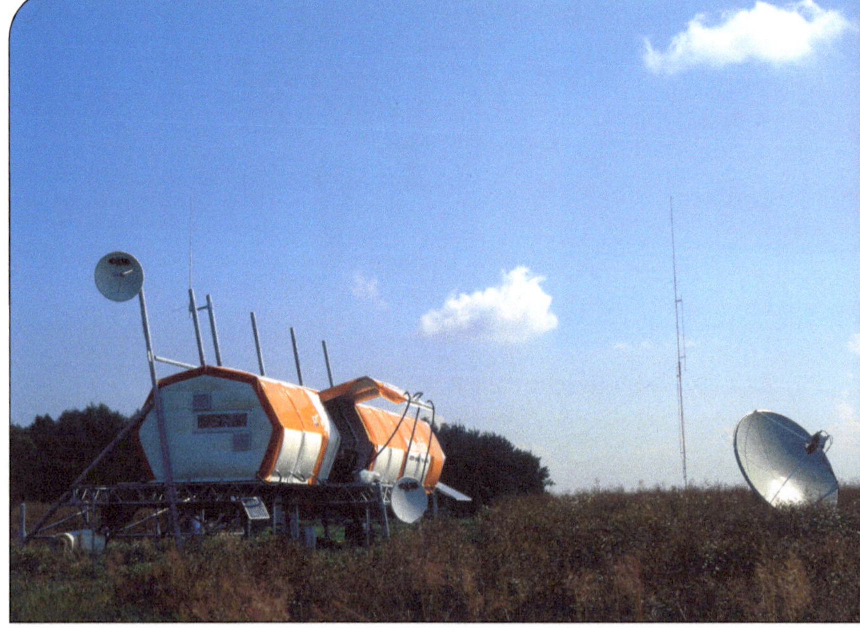

It's Documenta X, and a strange object has landed on Lutterberg Hill, 10 miles outside Kassel in the centre of Germany. Projekt Atol's MAKROLAB: a portable, weatherproof, self-sustainable 'insulation/isolation' environment perches between a grain field and a golf course, with a clear view of the town in the valley, and the strangely appropriate backdrop of a wind farm on the opposite hill. Like a figment of the late 20th century collective imagination, the scene is a vital and spirited visual quotation, bolted together from *2001: A Space Odyssey*, visionary architecture in the honourable tradition of Buckminster Fuller and Archigram, and the Constructivist love affair with the materials and aesthetics of science and technology.

MAKROLAB is the largest object in Documenta – this year an intellectually driven but still somehow bombastic statement on the state of contemporary art practice – and yet is also ironically the piece of work most dependent on time-based activity and complex, interlocking levels of mediation. The structure functions as a living and working environment, solar powered, and able to support 3 people for up to 40 days. Avowedly utopian in its objectives, the insulation/isolation strategy aims to achieve total independence from social conditions in order to create a reflective space. The object of reflection include "dreams, psychoacoustics, weather and low energy systems", but also "actual social conditions". This isolated 'no-place' therefore, is also thoroughly connected; through satellite receivers, microwave links, shortwave radio and, with its only physical link to the 'outside' world, an ISDN internet connection that trails 600 metres across the golf course.

Projekt Atol was founded in 1992, an initiative of Slovenian artist Marko Peljhan. He has spent the past five years, together with a team of young Slovenian hackers, bedroom engineers and radio hams, creating errant offspring of the military-industrial complex. Results so far: a film, *Ladomir: First Surface* (1994) – a meditation in colour, line and movement inspired by Vassily Kandinsky's *Bilder Einer Ausstellung*, made by a mixture of home-brewed programming and high-tech real-time graphic rendering. An installation, *Terminal* (1996), where aircraft navigation charts were projected in the gallery, with sound transmitted from scans of radio conversations between pilots and controllers as they negotiated the no-fly zones over the former Yugoslavia. *Urban Colonisation and Orientation Gear – 144* (1996), was an experiment overlapping psychogeography and communications technology, consisting of a number of group members wandering the streets of Ljubljana carrying home-made versions of the US military's GPS – global

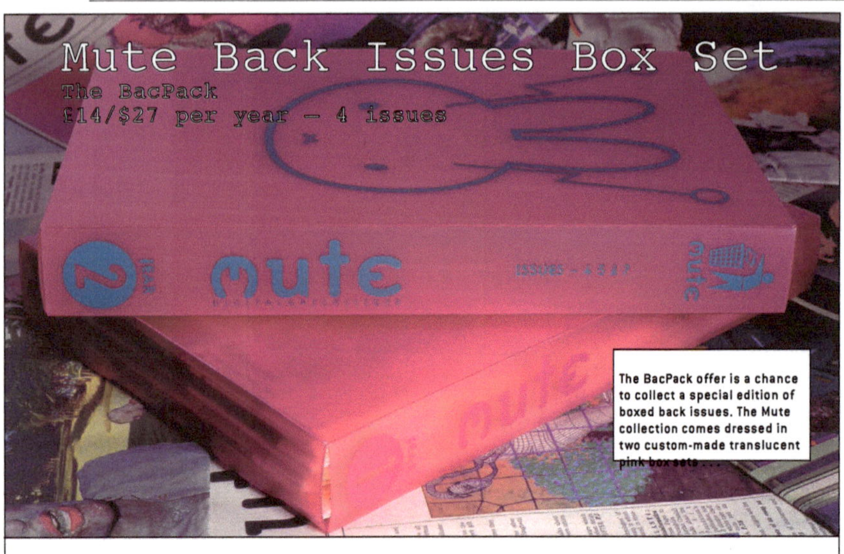

Year 1: issues pilot,1,2,3 (94-95) uk/eu £14 other £18/$27 inc p&p
Year 2: issues 4,5,6,7 (96-97) uk/eu £14 other £18/$27 inc p&p
credit card T +44(0)171 613 4743 F +44(0)171 613 4052 E: subs@metamute.com W: www.metamute.com/subs

positioning system – used together with wireless modems and audio receivers to create a collage of activity on the streets and on the net[1]. Plus there have beena prolific number of writings, performances and lectures.

MAKROLAB is the third and final manifestation of a cycle of projects called Ladomir – ФАКУРА, which pivot on the writings of the Russian Avant-Garde poet, Velimir Khlebnikov. His work, published in the 1920s, reads as a charming and irresistible mixture of archaic futurology and an uncannily contemporary vision. Khlebnikov mobilises a dense, deeply metaphorical and lyrical use of language (even in translation) to link natural phenomena with technologies and human inner life. His writing lurches from the wildly fantastic: "Grow edible microscopic organisms in lakes. Every lake will become a kettle of ready-made soup that only needs to be heated: contented people will lie about on the shores, swimming and having dinner" to the improbably incisive: "Let air travel and wireless communication be the two legs humanity stands on. And let's see what the consequences will be". The work *Ladomir*, published in 1922, takes its title from two Russian words, each with pointed double meanings: 'Lad' means both harmony and living creature. 'Mir' – as anybody who has spent any time in Russia will know – means both world and peace. Khlebnikov developed his own theory of language in which each letter of the alphabet is imbued with specific qualities, and in this system the joining letter 'o' is defined as "the letter which increases size".

However remote from this fanciful legacy the structure may seem at first glance, MAKROLAB is designed primarily to materialise these ideas – to build a processing device through which environmental, personal and communications activity is traced, structured, documented and re-presented. In a countervailing move to modern representation, the project concentrates on materialising the abstract, rather than abstracting the materiality of the everyday.

To this end, the lab aimed to work as a node within branching patterns of flows and processes through time and space – be they radio waves, weather patterns or bird migration. The clamouring, noisy, congested contents of the electro-magnetic spectrum was a special target, and one member of the team working as a guest researcher in the lab was US video maker, Brian Springer. During the 1992 US Presidential elections, Springer captured and recorded off-air satellite feeds of campaign broadcasts. The resulting film, *Spin*, makes a wry, revealing portrait of television, and politicians, in the making. While working at MAKROLAB Springer collaborated with Peljhan in experimenting with further satellite scanning activity, while investigating the legal frameworks of telecommunications interception, privacy and encryption. In the meantime, the minutiae of this peculiar daily existence was being recorded and various forms, and regular bulletins posted on a web site.

The MAKROLAB web site was just one of the multiple, multivalent, platforms through which people could maintain contact with the lab and experience something of it as an artwork. A console in the main gallery, the Documenta Halle, housed a live, microwave video feed from the lab, and a short-wave radio link for direct voice contact. The web site was accessible via a terminal there, and the crew in the lab received up to 20 emails each day. With the vast majority of communication consisting of questions stretching to little more than "what are you doing?" and "is this art?" it was difficult to be optimistic about the quality of casual visitors' experience of the work. However, for the dedicated it was quite possible to drive up and visit the lab, privileged few friends and colleagues stayed there for a number of days, and rumours circulated of gatherings on the site that back in the UK would have brought the police out in force under the Criminal Justice Act. A radio broadcast on Hessischer Rundfunk took place towards the end of the research project, and a key point in the process, undertaken 60 days into the project, was a lecture by Peljhan reflecting on the experience of this design for living, with its specificity of conditions and objectives, and operation through many kinds of communication media.

In its setting on Lutterberg hill, MAKROLAB carves out a point of calm and reflection within a cacophonic landscape of natural, urban, synthetic and technological processes. Adopting a cyborg strategy, it acts as a networking machine of experience, representation, environment, technology and communication as it maps out, records and re-distributes the invisible and powerful in airborne flows. It is a grandiose claim to materialise a utopia, or even to point towards what this might be. However, through its engagement with social and political realities, this is no call to simply tune in and drop out. By acknowledging both the inevitability and the use-value of mediation, and the non-innocence of the technology it uses, the project occupies a point of tension between the desirability and impossibility of physical and ethical autonomy. We are challenged to allow this tension to leak out from its isolated environment and put it to constructive, everyday work.

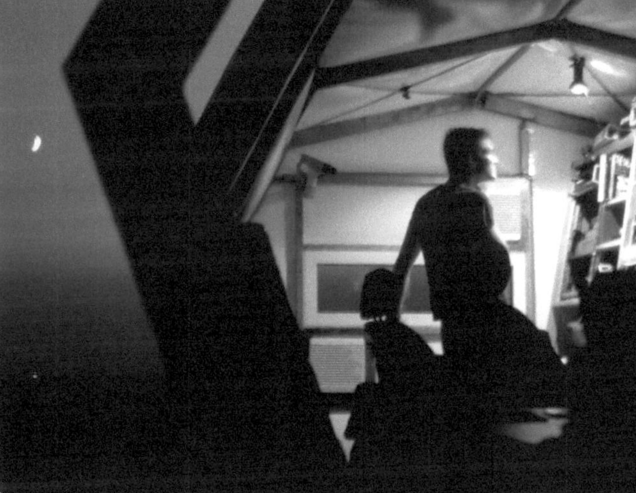

MAKROLAB crew: Luka Frelih, Bostjan Hvala, Borja Jelic, Jurij Krpan, Marko Peljhan, Brian Springer.MAKROLAB web site: [makrolab.ljudmila.org] includes details on future sites for the MAKROLAB project and the full text of Marko Peljhan's lecture for Documenta-X. An interview by Geert Lovink with Marko Peljhan and Brian Springer can be found on: [www.factory.org/nettime/archive/0912.html]

1 Matthew Fuller, "War Fever", *World Art Magazine*.

Photos MAKROLAB: Lisa Haskel, Kassel, 1997

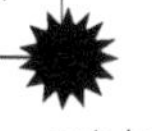

MARTIN MARTIN

Lying on her back, she gazes straight in your eyes. Child? Doll? Phantom? It's hard to tell. Motohiko Odani's photographic series *Phantom Limb* occupies a fitting – introductory – position in "Martin", a recent exhibition organised around the vampire theme of George Romero's film of the same name. *Phantom Limb* draws you past six photographs of a young Asian girlchild, with long black hair and arms spread out beside her body. Both her hands contain lumps of a red, fleshy substance. It seems she has been squeezing them. The only differences between the six photographs reside in her eyes and hands; they open – looking to the right; shut; open – looking directly at you; close – fingering the flesh-fruit. *Phantom Limb* was a fitting introduction because its crucifixion-like composition references religion more explicitly than any other work in the show, even though reflections on belief (of a sort) underlie all of them.

Martin – The Film – wears its vampire heart on its sleeve, but withholds the kind of narrative dénouement that might let you know whether it's 'truly' that of a vampire or not. Unlike the vampire films which exist to interpret the genre's 'commandments', Romero's *Martin* doesn't let you indulge in such structural certainties. In this respect, Romero's film, so 70s itself, prefigures the myriad vampire films of the 80s and 90s – many of which shifted away from the fixed notions of 'otherness' that hallmarked the genre before. (The 19th century, for example, produced vampires easily correlated with an ambient anti-semitism as well as more general anxieties to do with 'other' cultures and their increasing proximity via the ever more powerful vectors of travel, technology and Capital). The fact that Romero's Martin can easily touch garlic, walk around in the sunlight, handle crucifixes, etc. is just the tip of a doubt-inducing iceberg touching all aspects of his identity. Romero based his film on research into vampire sightings. The film, set firmly in the present, asks what kind of philosophical apparatuses we have to deal with such phenomena. Fundamentally, it is out to question *what* in Martin's behaviour, his sense of time, his relationships with other human beings, makes you assume that he is a vampire, or indeed human. Romero achieves this by casting doubt on the mental stability (read: normalcy) of *Martin* himself, but also on the notion that film, as a narrative medium with a specific cultural history and vantage points ensconced, could ever convey the 'truth' of any given situation. The fact that all of this is brought to bear via pretty obvious terms – i.e. 'magic', 'reality' etc. – belies the complexity of the film's conceits (as well as their adaptability to other discursive fields).

It is in this spirit of adaptability, or extrapolation – to the workings of Western culture and art – that the exhibition "Martin" was put together. It was curated by David Goldenberg and Taro Nasu and includes work by seventeen artists (from Britain, Ireland, Japan and Germany). "Martin's" aims are mightily ambitious, if not entirely new, ranging from a zeitgeisty attempt to break down the art object's autonomy to *representing* the cul-de-sacs of contemporary arts- and curatorial practice. "Martin" hopes to initiate a philosophical/theoretical thread at variance with both modernism and post-modernism for which, it argues, the cul-de-sacs of conservatism are more or less inbuilt. Using Romero's film as a starting point implicitly make rationality, time, history and identity central to the exhibition.

A hefty bite. And sometimes more than the curators could chew. The attempt to represent, critique *and* point in new directions was confusing, for example, as was the idea that the exhibition *itself* could embody a Heart-of-Darkness like movement from the light of convention and rationality into the heart of the repressed, breaking down "fixed bunkers of thinking and practice" in the process. The idea that one exhibition can straddle all of this handicapped it, and inaccurately presented some work as more radical than others (based, it seems, on more or less formal dictums). Although the combination of more and less 'conventionally' structured work produced some interesting relationships, surely we can't stand by those terms in any absolute sense. If anything, post-modernism should have taught us that there's more feeding into the 'bunkers of thinking' than what happens inside gallery walls. Thankfully, this was not "Martin's" primary theoretical aim. Neither was it easily deduced from the works themselves, so their mutual tensions remained ambiguous and interesting.

In the first site of the show – the Commercial Gallery – Florian Zeyfang's timeline of a Planet Hollywood opening provided a breakdown, plus photos, of one evening's event. Its dry notation of arrivals and departures, 'names' and linchpin figures ("Der Polizist", "Die Singerin", "Der Aktion Star" – Sylvester Stallone) applies a detective-like rigour to the evening's comings and goings, forcing the idea that such events merit obsessive and officious scrutiny. The whole exercise manages to perform an almost opera-like transformation on the evening. Perhaps there are invisible forces steering the proceedings? intent on orchestrating spectacles equal to those tracked by Rod Dickinson downstairs (*Crop Formation, Windmill Hill, Arebury Wiltshire, July 29 1996, Approx. 500H across*). Dickinson's now more familiar methods – collecting visual and written data from miscellaneous sources, including his own, on UFO sightings, crop circles and other unexplained phenomena – were followed, here and in the exhibition's other site, by childlike pencil drawings of UFO landings. Alison Gill's statuette *Receptor,* of a hooded Dr. Death figure with blood dripping down his body and arms, proved a heavy-handed counterpoint to her Kirlian photographs at Atlantis, while Rebecca Warren's *Upside Down* is an ode to an altogether more senior figure – its row of nines (i.e. sixes) requires little explanation.

In Atlantis' enormous space – the second and final destination – John Timberlake, Rebecca Warren and Fergal Stapleton placed works similar to those in the Commercial Gallery and not explicitly in keeping with the exhibition's theme (in Timberlake's case a series of cityscape paintings with clock faces telling different times; in Warren's and Stapleton's a continuation of their poetic, ephemeral and politely obtuse engagements with conceptual art). "Martin's" theme is so all-encompassing though that it's a case of the mountain/theme being able to come to Mohammed rather than Mohammed needing to go to the mountain.

Alasdair Duncan's *Untitled (The Young and the Beautiful)* was one of the most

Photo: "Martin", installation shot, Atlantis Gallery

light-hearted pieces in the show, but also one of the most haunting. Duncan acknowledged Robert Smithson's status as the show's éminence grise by using small dinosaurs (Smithson once described the dinosaurs on display at the Museum of Natural History as modern art works equal to any of those officially sanctioned by 'art' museumification). Duncan had placed his little clay dinosaurs on the ground – they looked like they'd been let loose and were ready to walk off. Behind them on the wall slapdash oil paintings on cardboard echoed their physical, slightly pathetic, forms. In the paintings each dinosaur stands gazing out majestically over habitats long lost.

Steven Wong's installation "Department of Titles. From the Teleological to the Heterogeneous, After Makunaima", engaged with history in a more 'scientific' way. The piece studiously mimics certain anthropological and criminological methodologies and incorporates them into a display of artefacts. "Department of Titles" hypothesises how these disciplines, among others, dovetail with the more 'elevated' spheres of Western culture – literature, art and architecture. It's a circular piece – moving back and forth between Western and non-Western cultures, 'real' and simulated archival objects – and avoids the didacticism similar projects often suffer from.

Orphan Drift's installation "You Its Eyes" is an older piece. Deliberately placed at the end of the exhibition, in "Martin's" planned 'Heart of Darkness', "You Its Eyes" doesn't require the curators' meta-discourse to pull you into its otherworldliness. Totally segregated from the rest of the exhibition in a blacked out room, you have to enter the piece through a side opening, smelling eucalyptus as you go in. Yes, sounds cheesy, but the video has the kind of melancholy beauty that keeps you from caring about presentational formalities. Watched in complete silence, it proves that 0.D>'s valorising of club culture and techno-music hasn't necessarily done them any favours. When allied to club-culture as a matter of course, 0.D>'s imagery seems overdetermined, sometimes even predictable. "You Its Eyes" silent surrounds demand a different kind of attention, and reward it amply. The video has been worked and reworked to the point where dissolution is always on the horizon. Viewing it means flitting in and out of a bleeding, congealing televisual world at speeds which come to feel anything but human. Perhaps that's the sensation Martin was getting at when he tried to tell his family what he felt like.

PvMB

'Martin', Commercial Gallery and Atlantis, 146 Brick Lane.
12th June – 9th July 1997

I won't promise you the earth

Marion Kalmus at Kettle's Yard

Marion Kalmus' recent show at Kettle's Yard contained both recent and new work. The sheer volume of work presented here threatens to overwhelm the modest circuit of spaces at Kettle's Yard, yet through careful planning and meticulous design the layout remains manageable. Photographs, slide dissolve installations, video and computer animations all seem to co-exist appropriately, bringing us a combination of observational irony, symbolism and epic narrative to a common point for contemplation. Whether it be playfully paranoid reflections on the game, Chinese Whispers (*Wildfire*) or the absurd irony of a Doctor and Disabled parking space seen and photographed side by side (*Doctor Disabled*), we are repeatedly shown moments of transformation where 'worst' becomes 'best' or more typically 'bad' becomes 'different bad.' To use such nonspecific terminology seems appropriate as the work itself operates on so many levels, encompassing intensely personal and painful moments of self portraiture and wider (almost existential) narratives that carefully implicate both artist and viewer while pushing the viewer to reevaluate and celebrate fundamental aspects of what it is to be human.

In *Well*, we watch the terrible plight of a woman forced underwater by fire and reduced to life support gasps for air. This is a narrative of epic proportion rendered by clattering and jerkily dissolving slides. The self consciousness of the mechanics used in *Well* remove us so far from the story's endless horror that it has little more impact than a saying like "out of the frying pan and into the fire." However, to look no further than a cliché seems to underestimate the conceptual sophistication of Kalmus' work. Perhaps this sophistication is more evident in *Patient*, a new work using a computer and data projector to backproject a piece of text onto two strip-like screens placed side by side and embedded into the gallery wall. The sentence is scrambled and slowly revealed by going through the alphabet at every point until each letter, space or symbol is reached before moving on. The effect is somewhat similar to various startup and sorting procedures seen on many computer platforms, but slowed down by a magnitude reminiscent of Douglas Gordon's *24hour Psycho*. The text reads:

"It's worth remembering that a cube packed with touching spheres still has space in which smaller spheres can freely travel. So we can reach our destinations by patiently looking for the channels that others don't see; whether it's their method of transport or fixed opinions that are creating the traffic jams."

This ambiguous statement allows for a broad range of psychological, philosophical or scientific readings, obscured by the mimicked reconstruction of computer processes. It is in this work that Kalmus really seems to strike a compelling balance between her formal concerns and the stories she tells. An aesthetic beauty derived from the very processes driving the installation, underpinning a narrative that *can* be and is as much about the artist as ourselves.

Jon Thomson

Marion Kalmus, I won't promise you the earth, Kettle's Yard, Cambridge,

4th October – 9th November 1997

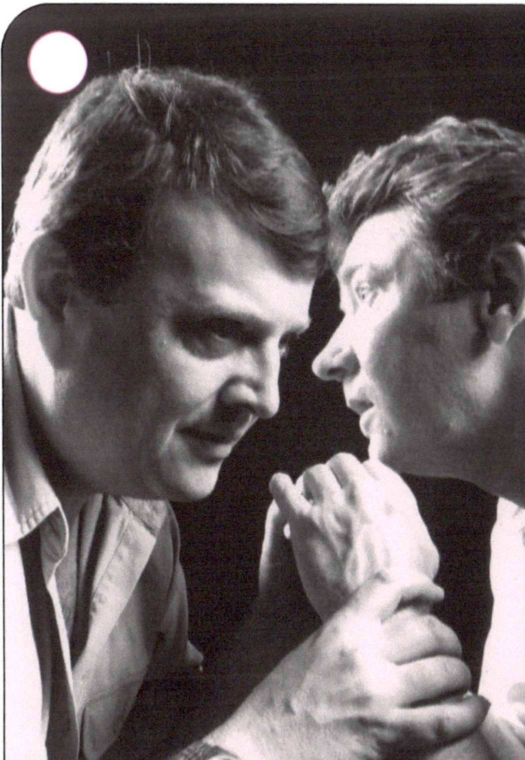

Marion Kalmus, No. 8 of 10, from *Wildfire*, 1997, Kettle's Yard

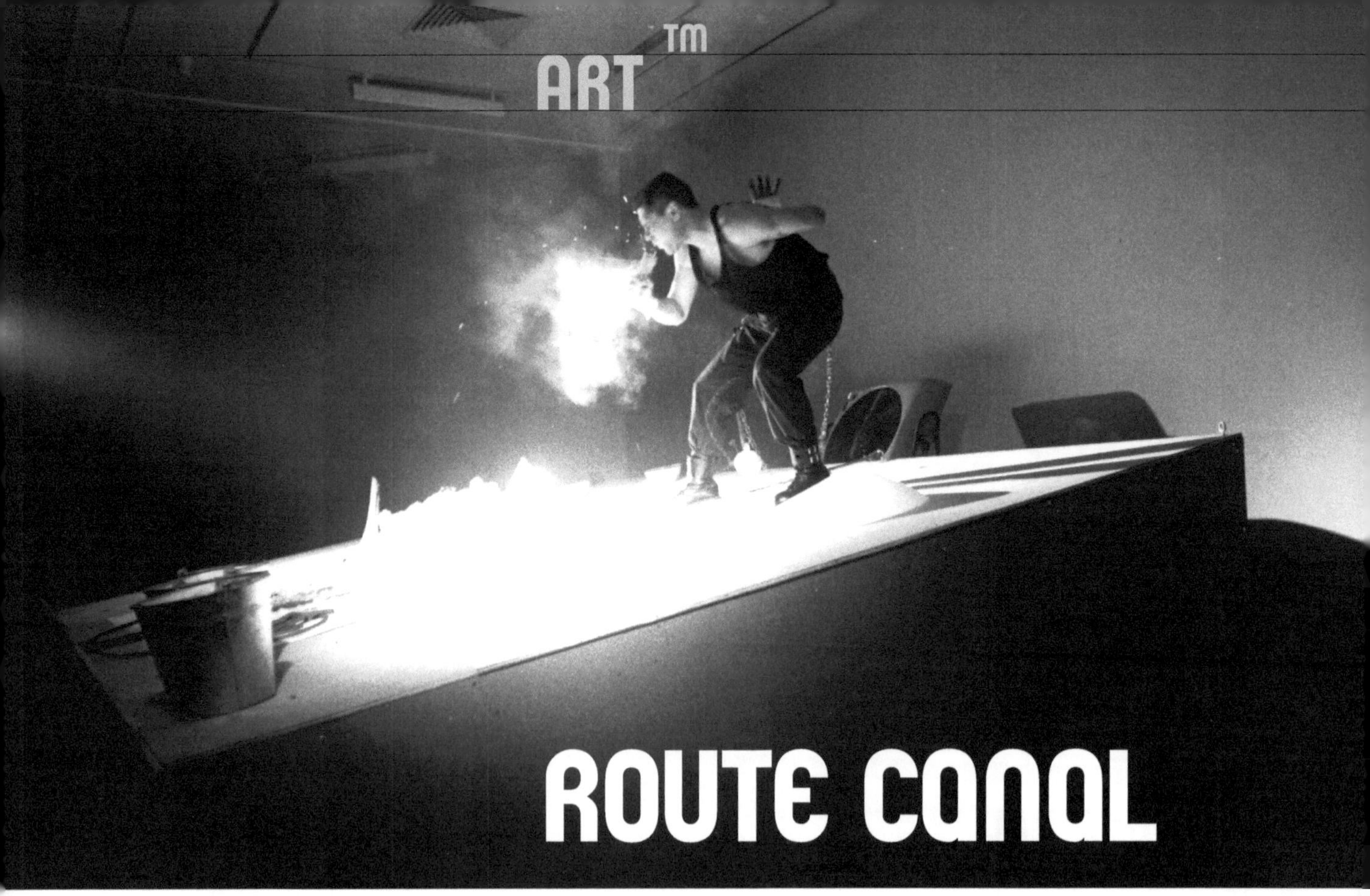

ROUTE CANAL

rootLESS'97 has been 'running out of time' again in Hull throughout October. With its punning, allusive title, the event is described as an International Festival of Live and Time Based Art. It feels like a frantic countdown to the year 2000, which is no doubt much as the organisers would wish.

Originally a child of Hull Time Based Arts, ROOT has always been an umbrella for different forms of live and virtual performance work. Like the NOW and eXpo events, which run annually in Nottingham, and the Youngblood '97 international theatre festival at the Green Room, Manchester, also November, ROOT offers a consumers' guide to the current avant garde. ROOT is the only one of these events in the UK that offers the artists and performers who are the avant garde a chance to look at one another and where they are going. Participating artists are booked into Hull for the whole event. Tight programming concentrates events in a 'Hot Weekend' (this year Friday-Sunday, Oct. 10-12), and the three or four main venues are within easy walking distance in Hull's compact city centre.

Within ROOT'97, one discrete unit was the ATLAS symposium (11 Oct., Spring Street Theatre). ATLAS (Archive for Transnational Living Art Studies) (re)united speakers from performance archives in England, Germany, Hungary, Québec, and Switzerland. The English Arts Council is currently attempting to track the disappearing history of performance art, and some of us who were there at the beginning (the 60s) are submitting to belated attempts to catch us on film/video before it is too late. It has recently become fashionable to academicise hybrid forms like performance art. Has the spirit of post- (or super-) modernism broken out of the sanitary cordon the universities had built around it? woven from an impenetrable language and sterile discourses. After a spate of conferences on situationism, and self-contradictory Fluxus retrospectives, performance (art) just had to be re-discovered, where it has always been, at the heart of modern culture. The Nomad Domain was another large section of ROOT'97, sub-titled "Provocative art works from specially commissioned international participants from Europe and North and Central America". If this sounds like routine artspeak, consider: "The ignorant are tied to their native land, the mediocre consider themselves citizens of the world, but only the wise realise they are a stranger everywhere", *Lo Straniero journal*, motto. Lo Straniero (The Stranger) is a generic name for a number of itinerant artists who occasionally surface to run 'interventions'. They also feature in long printed address lists, constructed to give the impression that 'they' are everywhere, but rarely where you would expect them – in art galleries. Lo Straniero's motto appeared in the ROOT'97 publicity, and gives a good feel of the glue that holds so many performance artists from different locations together, and impels them to meet to perform live.

The Nomad Territories were inaugurated in Québec, 1994; in part an expression of francophone and post-colonial separatism. Members of the Territories carry realistic passports, issued through consuls in different states and based on the traditional UK 'Britannic Majesty' model. The Co-General consuls of the Nomad Territories for England are Julie Bacon and Roddy Hunter, both Hull-based performance artists who travel widely – organisers of The Nomad Domain.

Andre Stitt, *At Climax*, rootLESS'97
Photo: Hull Time Based Arts

Travelling features in the history of performance art as a political necessity. In the 50s and 60s artists in Hungary and Czechoslovakia would cross their national borders to escape the censorship that came with the Red Army's invasions. In the 70s and 80s Poland offered a freer environment for artists from other communist countries. And throughout the Cold War, artists who could, came to what we naively called the 'Free West'. The art work as object, as text, film or tape, was difficult to smuggle across a hostile border. Artists carrying their works inside their heads (improvising performers) were more likely to escape the attentions of customs and immigration officials. Today, economic wars having taken over from ideological ones, marginalised people (Slovak Romanies, New Age Travellers, migrant workers) are the ones seeking freedom from persecution; close relatives of performance artists, their intellectual property is in their heads, hands, and feet.

Artists in many situations live outside regular economic structures, creating goods and services that have to find their own market, for which there may be no pre-existing demand. Artists, as a class, are marginal in many societies. The nomad, the traveller, is a natural role model.

Many of the artists presenting performances in ROOT'97 were self-declared members of the Nomad Territories, some are consuls. The Nomad Territories is not the first attempt at a stateless nationality. Neoism?! in the late 70s, and Jim Haynes (founder of the original London Arts Lab in the 60s) produced stateless passports – it is an honourable tradition.

A quick, flip-through guide to some of the ROOT'97 artists shows how they connect: Julie Bacon's *mgh and 1/2mv2* was a series of actions marking the boundaries of Hull Paragon rail station and tracks. Jackie Chettur created a film/video viewing space inside a silver Citroen CX estate car, *The Silver Dream Machine*, parked outside Warehouse 6, a sand-blasted memorial to the days when Hull was a thriving port. Between Warehouse 6 and the Ferens Gallery is Princes Quay – a shopping development in what used to be a dock, that gives meaning to the phrase 'Dead in the Water'.

Brian Connolly's *History Lesson* was an installation inside the Ferens Gallery that held fragments of historical imagery in a web of light. Phil Coy's *Departure* brought together the Icarus myth and hitch-hiking, local pigeon fanciers and a live projected video of domestic arrangements set in the Ferens Gallery's 'Live Art Space'. In *Otiose*, John Dummett and Ailith Roberts pursued slow and laborious researches into the matter of the Gallery's Centre Court, at one point using fingerprint dusting techniques on the marble floor. In *Die Wandersmann/The Wanderer*, performed in Warehouse 6, Ronald Fraser-Munro used pre-filmed video sequences, monologues, and his own oddly androgynous figure (long blond wig, black skin, military greatcoat). His subjects were fugitives, ghosts, inhabitants of the spiritual diaspora. Also in Warehouse 6, Rob Gawthorp (with Gina Czarnecki) in *Percussion Video and Noise* mixed hilarious mechanical toys – 'talking parrots' – smart remote control video at table top level, and his own live drum solo. Guillermo Gómez-Pena and Roberto Sifuentes performed *The Mexterminator* in the Ferens Gallery – a 'tableaux vivant' which illustrated and challenged the conventional image of the Mexican – bullets, guns, chickens, drugs and mustaches.

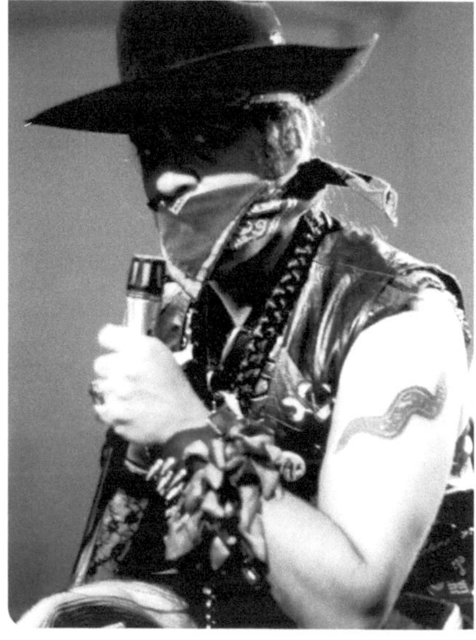

Istvan Kantor (also known by the generic name Monty Casin) calls himself the initiator, in the 70s, of Neoism?! – a "nomadic, anti-authoritarian pseudo-philosophy". His concert/performance *Executive Travel* deployed computer-choreographed hydraulically powered filing cabinets to create high level noise. Rona Lee's *Present* was in Beverley Art Gallery, an early 20th century building where she sat attempting to draw the perfect circle. Her drawings were given to the gallery, making a sharp commentary on the relationship between donations to the Permanent Collection and the Public.

Simon Lewandowski's *The Migrating Machine* was a futile, plodding robot, manoeuvring clumsily around Warehouse 6. Richard Martel performed *Étude ethnologique avec grand piano* in one of the Ferens galleries, applying a severed ox tongue to his own face and to the heads of portraits on the gallery walls. His thesis was that *la langue* (tongue, language), was the performative, articulating the silenced. André Stitt in *At Climax* violently and noisily attacked his favourite range of materials – wet, sticky, powdery – on a sloping wooden ramp in another Ferens space, with a pile of ice and a model of the Titanic in the foreground. Artur Tajber's *3 Desolation* drew the audience into the cramped confines of the Red Gallery, near a pub where, on the Sunday evening, pretend gunslingers in cowboy hats and boots gathered. *3 Desolation* involved a TV monitor, which Taiber carried on his shoulder, a curiously inscribed white hood over his head, like the drawing of a brain, and some low tunnels through which he crawled. The performance was long and occupied three different sites. Valentine Torrens' untitled performance, in Warehouse 6, used darkness, luminous paint applied to the wet walls, a tennis-ball serving machine that shot luminous balls at the spectators, projections of riot control incidents, and a harrowing sound track. Torrens, who wore a black hood, ended in one corner, propped by his forehead against the wall. On the ground floor of Warehouse 6, Ann Whitehurst in her wheel chair created messages in bottles which were thrown into the nearby dock. She also used the internet in her performance *Current Movements*, which was subtitled:

"Stranger than a Stranger
For Those Disabled People
Excluded in every century
Excluded in every culture"

Roland Miller

Guillermo Gómez-Pena and Roberto Sifuentes, *Mexterminator*, rootLESS'97
Photo: Hull Time Based Arts

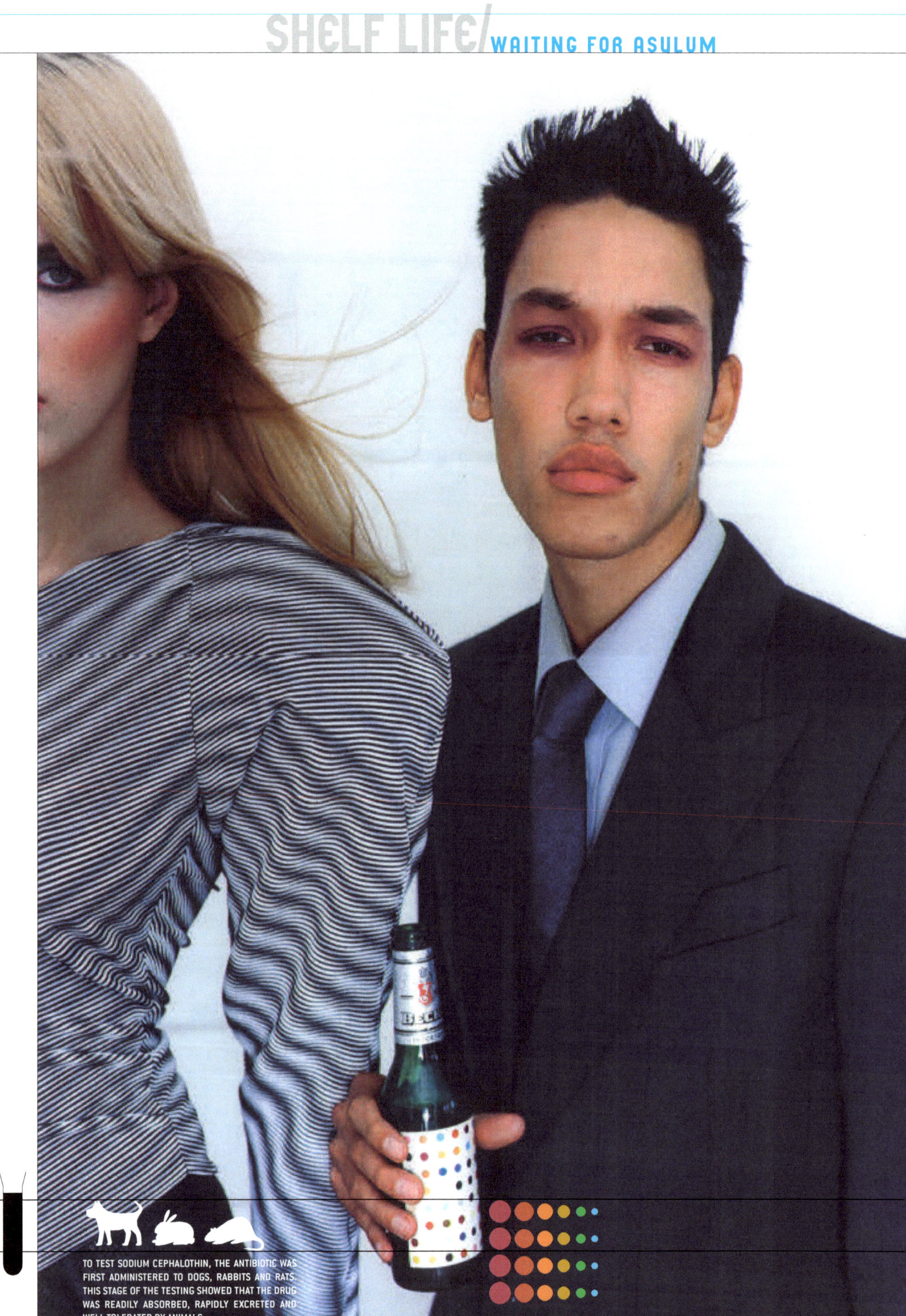

TO TEST SODIUM CEPHALOTHIN, THE ANTIBIOTIC WAS FIRST ADMINISTERED TO DOGS, RABBITS AND RATS. THIS STAGE OF THE TESTING SHOWED THAT THE DRUG WAS READILY ABSORBED, RAPIDLY EXCRETED AND WELL TOLERATED BY ANIMALS.

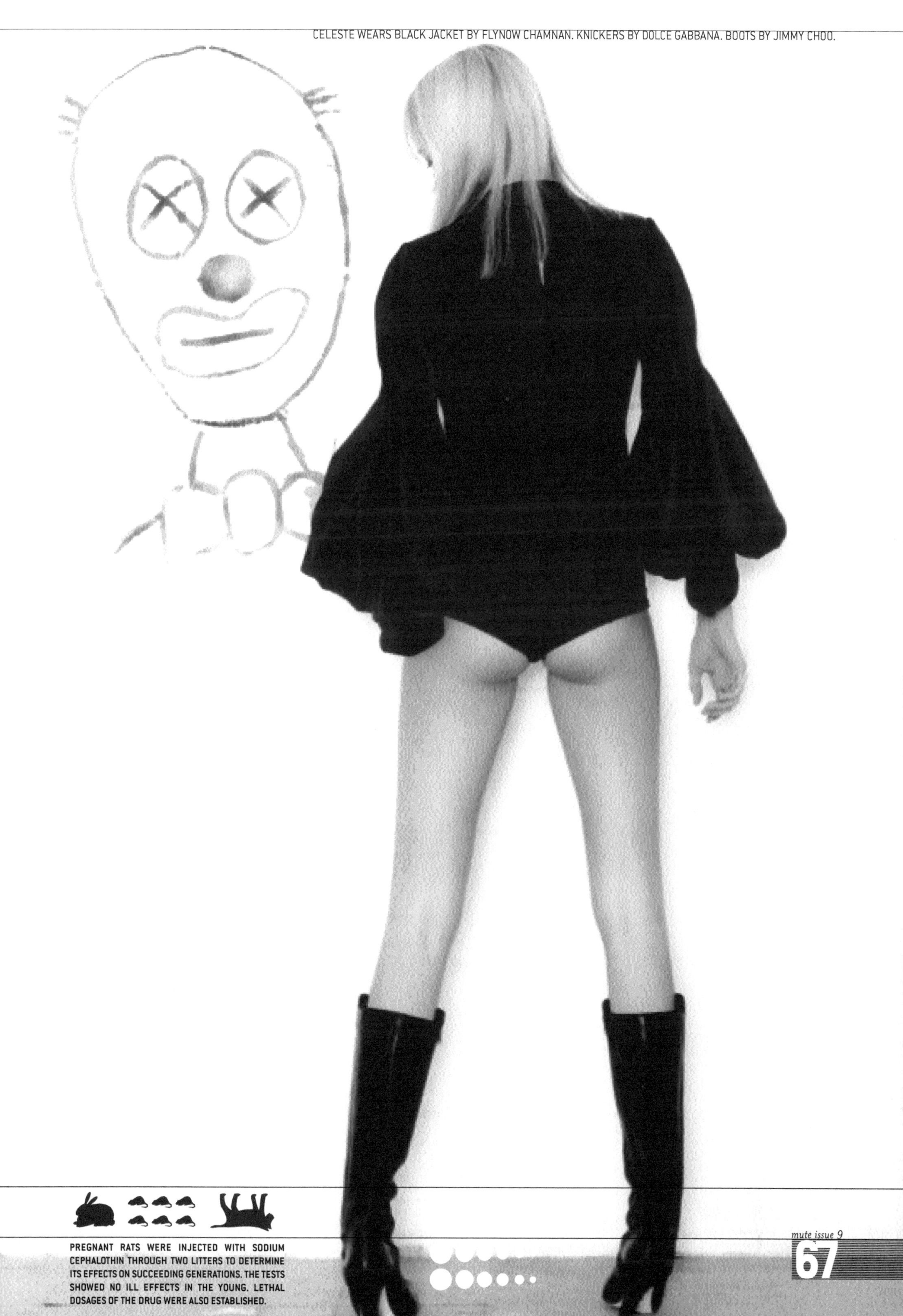

CELESTE WEARS BLACK JACKET BY FLYNOW CHAMNAN. KNICKERS BY DOLCE GABBANA. BOOTS BY JIMMY CHOO.

PREGNANT RATS WERE INJECTED WITH SODIUM CEPHALOTHIN THROUGH TWO LITTERS TO DETERMINE ITS EFFECTS ON SUCCEEDING GENERATIONS. THE TESTS SHOWED NO ILL EFFECTS IN THE YOUNG. LETHAL DOSAGES OF THE DRUG WERE ALSO ESTABLISHED.

MELODY WEARS CUSTOMISED NURSE DRESS FROM ALEXANDRA. TIGHTS BY CALVIN KLEIN. SHOES BY RED OR DEAD.

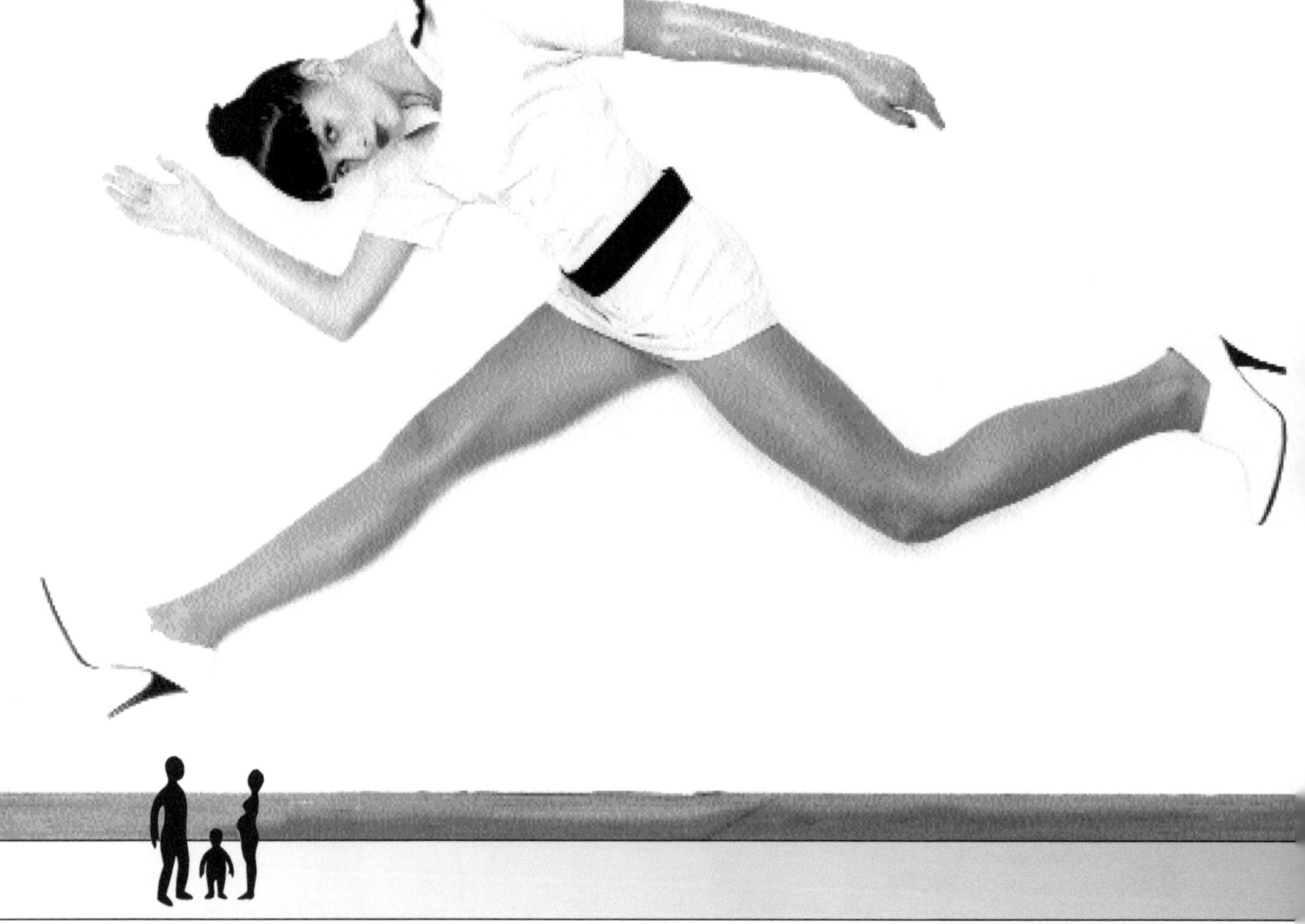

ADULTS, PREGNANT WOMEN AND CHILDREN WERE GIVEN THE DRUG. IT WAS EASILY ABSORBED, RAPIDLY EXCRETED AND WELL TOLERATED, CONFIRMING EARLIER ANIMAL TESTS.

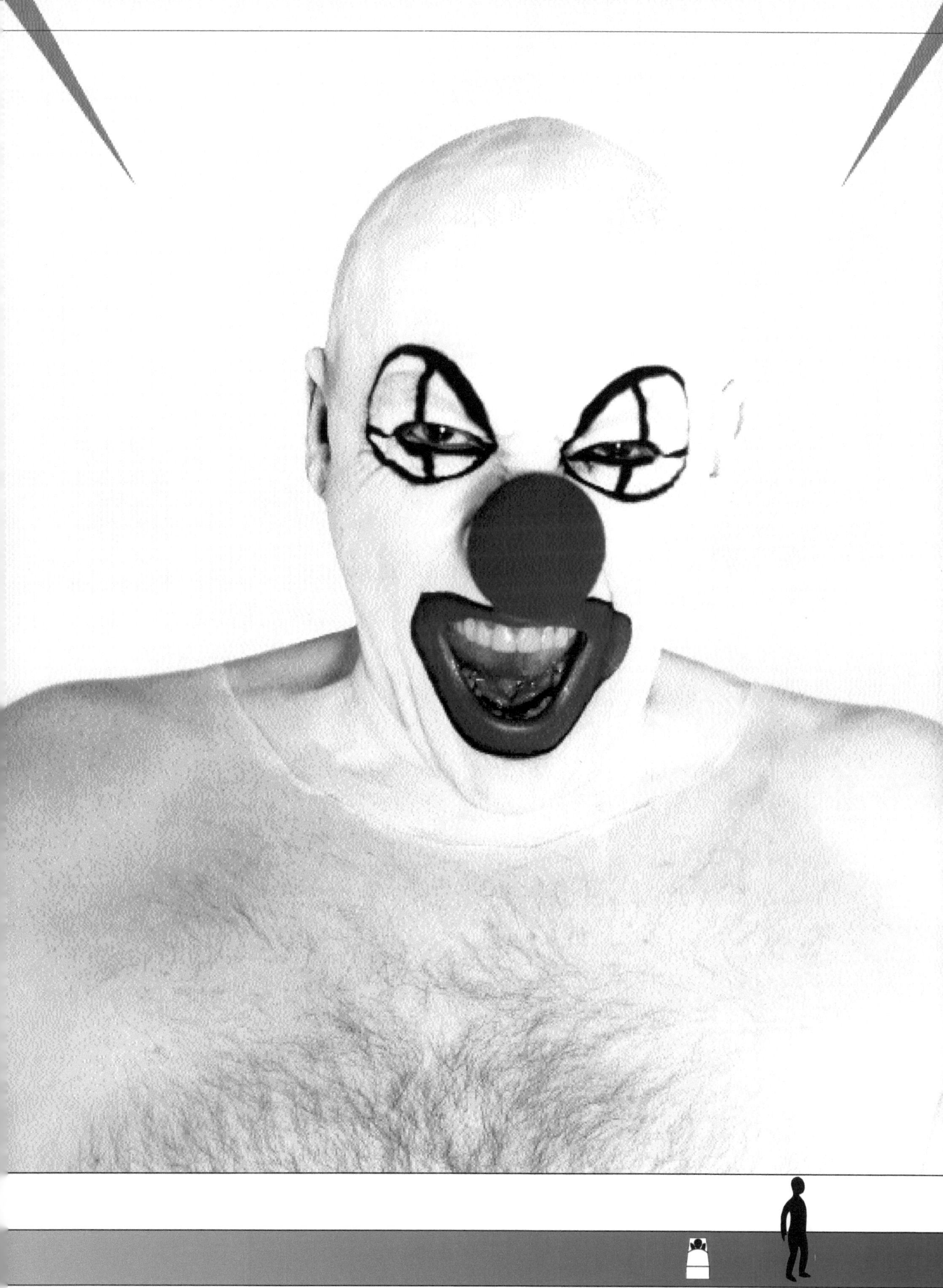

CHILDREN AND ADULTS WERE INJECTED WITH VARYING AMOUNTS OF THE DRUG AND APPROPRIATE DOSAGES WERE ESTABLISHED.

MELODY DRESS AS BEFORE. BOOTS BY JIMMY CHOO.
CELESTE WEARS BEADED SHOULDER PIECE BY DARREN MATTHEW'S TO ORDER ON 0370 387 400. SKIRT BY PIERCE FIONDA.
SHOES FROM THE CONTEMPORARY WARDROBE AS BEFORE.

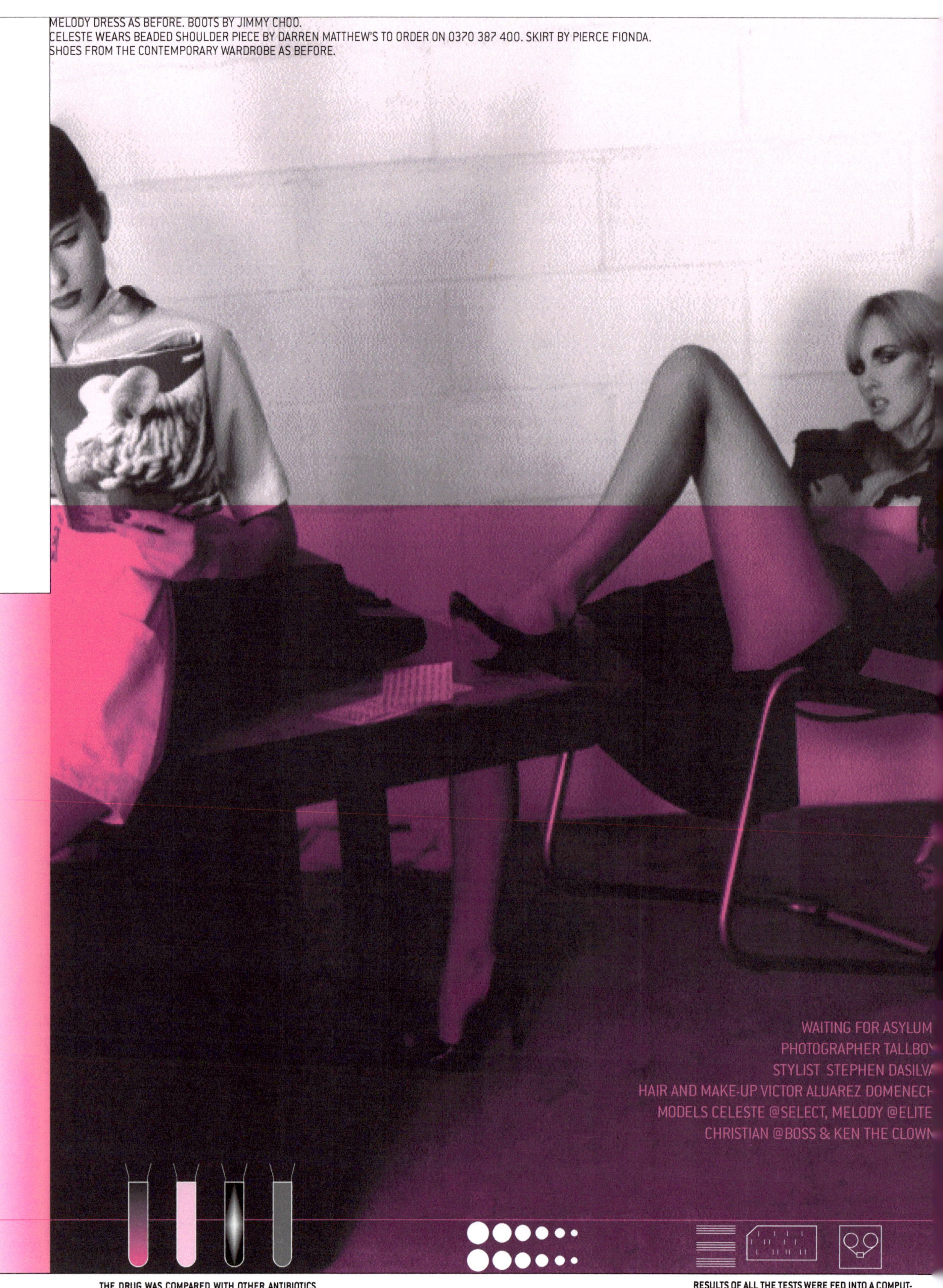

THE DRUG WAS COMPARED WITH OTHER ANTIBIOTICS FOR EFFECTIVENESS SO THAT IT COULD BE ASSIGNED ITS PROPER PLACE IN COMBATING INFECTION.

RESULTS OF ALL THE TESTS WERE FED INTO A COMPUTER. THIS INFORMATION WAS THEN SENT TO THE U.S. FOOD AND DRUG ADMINISTRATION, AND APPROVAL OF THE DRUG FOLLOWED ANALYSIS OF THE DATA.

ISSUE 10 OUT APRIL 1998.
COPY DEADLINE: 7 MARCH
contents ø1415 g

DIGITAL STUDIES: BEING IN CYBERSPACE is an online event for new media art and theory co-organized by mark amerika and alex galloway. EXHIBITION GOALS: > cyborg-narrators > html conceptualism > navigational aesthetics > networked intelligentsia > self-transmission radio > open(BOMB, ">>$la bombe"); > ARTificial life > typographical disembodiment (the layered-effect) > prophetic nerves...
[www.altx.com/ds]

Eclecticism gets a dusting down at this year's **Music Alliance**, where FUTUREsonic will be helping stage a series of discussions, technical demonstrations and music showcases exploring all corners of the sonic spectrum, from jazz to world to electronic. Of particular interest are the Arts of Technology and Remix Culture panels. 6-8 March 98, The Barbican, Spitz and Vibe Bar.
Xmusicalliance@blissful.demon.co.ukX T: 0181 372 9735.

EYE OF THE STORM: Artists in the Maelstrom of Science
Announcing a major international art and science conference and series of evening debates, organised by The Arts Catalyst at the Royal Institution, Piccadilly, London, UK.
Some of the major controversies in modern science will be discussed with eminent scientists and artists from various media discussing and debating the issues. Scientists include Roger Penrose (author of The Emperor's New Mind), Ian Wilmut from the Roslin Institute (progenitors of Dolly the Sheep), Jack Cohen (author of The Collapse of Chaos), Heinz Wolff, Sheila MacLean and Lewis Wolpert. Artists include Stelarc (Aus), Kathy Acker (US), James L Acord (US) and zero-gravity choreographer Kitsou Dubois (F).
Maelstrom conference 19 & 20 Feb 1998
Eye of the Storm evening debates 3, 10, 17 & 24 Feb 1998
Co-chairing the Maelstrom conference will be Melvyn Bragg and Susan Greenfield.

CONTACT: The Arts Catalyst, 28A Brightwell Crescent,
London SW17 9AE
X supanova@artscat.demon.co.uk X
[www.artscat.demon.co.uk]

'Getting On-line - An Internet Guide for Arts Organisations' by Gary Wiltshire, an RABs publication, explains basic principles of the Internet; case studies of how arts organisations are making use of the Internet and a listing of Internet Service Providers and Cybercafe sites in Britain. It's available free from the your local RABs Information department.
Tel: 01924 455555 X yharts-info@geo2.poptel.org. X

Lovebytes Digital Arts Festival 23/5. April 98.
Open Call for Digital Film/ Video Audio and Multimedia.
If you produce film/ video, audio or multimedia using computers and digital processes this is your opportunity to get it shown. If selected, your work will be featured as part of an extensive programme at the Sheffield Media and Exhibition Centre, exploring new media technologies, alongside a conference exploring 'digital art' through critical debate.
Open Free Entry: Deadline 14 January 1998.
Tel +44 (0) 114 221 0393
Xlovebyte@syspace.co.ukX
[www.lovebyte.org.uk]

Opportunity to adopt!
One year ago, in July, '96, I made "On se comprend" ("we understand each other") [www.cicv.fr/on_se_comprend.html] at CICV (Centre International de Creation Video) in France. It was done, but it is not definitive, it is not yet finished at this time. So, now, and with CICV's agreement, I'd like to entrust this work to somebody else. Somebody who will take care of it and let it evolve. The idea is to let it continue its own way, to have other mirror sites linked (2 are still open to receive other translations)."On se comprend" can move and change languages and sites with a new manager. A suggestion: one could take charge of "On se comprend" for one year only.
Keep in touch: [www.cicv.fr/on_se_comprend.html]
From: Antoine Moreau Xantomoro@imaginet.frX

store in a cool,dry place away from sunlight

THE VIRTUAL BERET PROJECT
The Virtual Beret Project was begun in 1994 by Sarah Smiley, and currently has over 150 archived "virtual artists." Invent your own!
[www.ariel.com.au/VirtualBeret]
or Xssmiley@tiac.netX for more info.

EUROPEAN MEDIA ART FESTIVAL, May 6-10, Germany.
Over 140 experimental films & videos, as well as computer & video installations. CD-ROM, text contributions & Internet projects showcased at this fest, one of largest annual events for innovative & experimental works in those fields. Open to "experiments, to the extraordinary, to all those working methods which, using the most diverse media. create intelligent, radical or ironic worlds of symbols & signs in today's digital age." All film & video works must have been completed w/in previous yr. Awards go to best German experimental film or video prod. Best of cat media awards. In special programs, current political, societal & artistic topics explored. An int'l student forum, retros, workshops & open air events are also held. Appl. for installations, expanded media & exhibition projects should enclose detailed calculation of costs, precise description, photo material & video documentation if possible. Site for installations is art gallery Dominikanerkirche. >>Selected films/ videos compensated w/ DM40/minute with a minimum of DM40 & maximum DM 160. >>No entry fee (but return of preview material requires DM 20).
DEADLINE: 2nd of March 1998. Formats: 35mm, 16mm, 3/4", 1/2", S-8, Beta, 8mm, installations, Internet. CD-ROM. Entry fee: None.
CONTACT: Alfred Rotert, Director, European Media Art Festival, PO. Box 1861, Lohstrasse 45a, D-49008 Osnabruck, Germany;
tel. 49/ 541/ 21658; fax: 28327; Xemaf@bionic.zerberus.deX
[www.emaf.de]

intima virtual base - creative intimate lab
[www2.arnes.si/ffljintima2]
free your mind and the rest will follow

MITES (Moving Image Touring & Exhibition Service) is running a series of short training courses offering professional opportunities for artists and exhibitors to understand the creative applications of new technologies.
NEW TOOLS+ New Tools+ builds on the experience of five years of support for artists and exhibitors through MITES and the original New Tools programme. Aimed squarely at the current and future needs of artists, curators and gallery staff, the courses offer supportive and informative routes into understanding the creative applications of new media technologies.
•Dealing with Exhibition Technology - 11 Nov 1997 & 17 Feb 1998 (1 day) /£40. •Multimedia in the Gallery - 12 Nov 1997 & 18 Feb 1998 (1 day) / £40. •Networked Art - 25 November 1997 (1 day) / £40. •Starting with Computers for Artists - 2,3,4 Dec 1997 (3 days) / £100. •Multimedia for Artists - 20,21,22 January 1998 (3 days) / £100. •Breakers - 4 February 1998 (sessions) free •Interactive Catalogue Design - 3,4,5 March 1998 (3 days) / £100
CONTACT: Simon Bradshaw: MITES/FACT, Bluecoat Chambers, School Lane, Liverpool L1 3BX. T:0151 707 2881 / F: 0151 707 2150
X mites@fact.co.uk X

VW 98
CALL FOR PAPERS AND PARTICIPATION
This interdisciplinary conference aims to provoke new understandings of the important role that virtual worlds will play in domains such as business, computer games, education, training, simulation, etc. It will investigate the relationships between the natural and the artificial from both theoretical and philosophical points of views.

ART NEWS

ART NEWS IS A NON-COMMERCIAL, EDITED BULLETIN BOARD. RST COME / RSTSERVE. SMALL & INDEPENDENTS GET TO SKIP THE QUEUE.

PAPERS SUBMISSIONS
The papers will receive three independent reviews. The papers describing strong original research works will be accepted for publication in the conference proceedings, which will be also published as a book. Paper presenting less mature work will be presented at the conference but will not be published in the proceedings. Papers should not be longer than 12 pages, including title, names of authors and their addresses, email, and an abstract of 70-150 words. "Papers should be send to the Conference Secretariat (hard-copies) or to the conference chair (email)."
IMPORTANT DATES
Submission deadline : 28.2.1998/ Notification of acceptance : 4.98 / Camera-ready due : 5.1998 /Conference : July 1-3, 1998
STEERING COMMITEE: Conference Chair: Jean-Claude HEUDIN (IIM, France) XJean-Claude.Heudin@devinci.frX Conference Secretary: Sylvie PERRET (IIM, France) XSylvie.Perret@devinci.frX

European Media Art Residency Exchange
EMARE – residency for artist in media in Germany, Britain, Finland and Hungary. The 4th European Media Art Residency Exchange will take place in Summer/ Autumn 1998.
Artists in media (digital media, internet, film/photography/video, etc...) from Great Britain can apply for residencies with one of the other partner organisations. Duration of the scholarship: 1-2 month
LOCATIONS: Hull Time Based Arts, Kingston Upon Hull, UK/ Muu Media Base, Tornio, Lappland/ Werkleitz Gesellschaft, Saxony – Anhalt (village of Werkleitz near Dessau and Magdeburg) Germany. Scholarship: per month approx. 2.000,- DM
DEADLINE for participation forms: 31.01.98
Further information about proposal forms and guidelines:
HTBA • 8 Posterngate • Hull • HU1 2JN • UK T: 01482 216 446
Xhtba@htba.demon.co.ukX

The German/English net-magazine TELEPOLIS* [www.heise.de/tp] offers netspace for creative people who want to present their work in an environment of quality content and on a site which is well visited. All works which are genuinely made for the web – i.e. no documentation of other works – of a visual, text based, sound or mixed character are welcome. Selection of works will be made on the basis of individual judgement by the editors – no juries, no prizes, no money. The netspace functions as a showcase to aggregate interest. Intellectual property rights stay with the originators of the work (unless negotiated differently).

***Telepolis** has recently opened up an office in London, UK. Please send press releases, invitations for cyber-cultural events (plus chocolate and money) and submissions for netspace to Armin Medosch, 52B Andrews Rd., London E8 4RL, UK,
X armin@easynet.co.ukX

SEND EMAIL, HARD COPY OR FAX TO MUTE EDITORIAL ADDRESS (SEE CONTENTS). NO MORE THAN 55.3372 WORDS OR YOU GET THE CHOP.

XMUTE@METAMUTE.COMX

In the cutting edge tradition you have come to know and love, *Mute* has developed a 3D art listings guide. Simply cut along the solid lines carefully with a pair of scissors, a very sharp scalpel or a clove of garlic. Fold along dashed lines and stick tabs to adjoining face with an adhesive of your choice.When completed you can read the listings whilst watching your favorite television programme or view the passing scenery from the comfort of a bus seat. *–Mr. Pleasure*

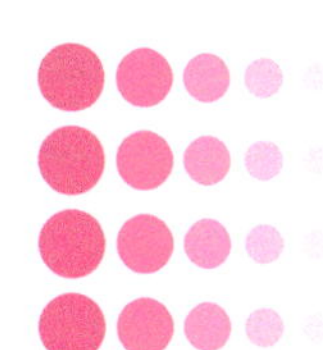

Modems and Bodums

The genteel setting of 15 Golden Square near Piccadilly Circus, a seemingly unlikely hangout for pirates, is indeed the place where they webcast their tunes around the world. This address is the home and 'community' of the Global Cafe. As well as providing standard cyber-services like expensive net access, cheap email accounts, good food, licensed bar, training, conferencing and business solutions, they also play host to 'The Global Channel' Pirate Radio [www.pirate-radio.co.uk] which grew out of InterFACE, the world's first pirate radio on the net, and plays from 17.00-00.00 Sunday through to Friday. So far they have navigated the seas to terminals in Japan, Europe, South America and Australia and received audience figures of over 80,000 a day.

Global to the last, there are many international DJ's that play here. As for the music, Plug (creator of 'The Global Channel' pirate radio) comments: "It never has the same style twice and therefore isn't governed by any scene". For those who need scene names (I did ask) Mix Master Morris, Colin Dale, Jumping Jack Frost, 4 Hero, Clear Records, Patrick Forge and Doctor Rockit have all played here. 'The Global Channel' is a non-commercial site – all costs are covered by those who play in this utopian, 'non-chin-scratching' event.

-Alison Bell

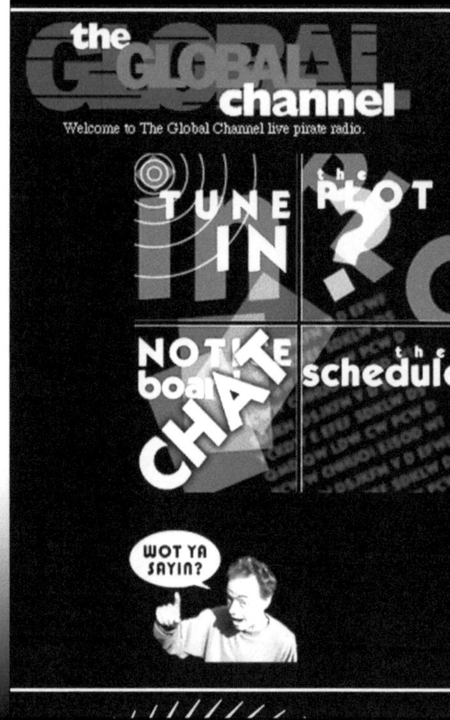

BUY YOUR MUTE AT THE FOLLOWING OUTLETS

CAFÉ NAME	TOWN	ADDRESS	OPENING HOURS	GADGETRY	GASTRONOMY	ATMOSPHERE & ADDITIONALS
the bean	London	126 Curtain Rd EC2A 3PL T:01717397829 E:bean1@hitsnet.com	8am-6pm Mon-Fri, 10am-4pm Sat-Sun	Basic Internet access	Continental pastries, healthy salads, sand-wiches, and a cornucopia of caffeinated solutions.	Art exhibitons, designer bean-bags (by Abi Partridge) heaps of magazines & techno-hip-hop-soul sounds."chilled out atmosphere & damn fine coffee!"
Café Internet	Liverpool	28 North John St T:0151 255 1112 E:cafe01@mail.mersinet.co.uk	10am-6pm Mon-Fri, 9am-6pm Sat, closed Sun	10 Pentium P120s, 128K ISDN line, networked games, colour printing.	Full range of coffees, teas, soft drinks and fresh sandwiches, hot snacks & pastries.	Internet Tuition, themed events, available for hire. "600 ft² of relaxed atmosphere and charming staff"
Café Internet	London	22-24 Buckingham Palace Rd SW1 W0OP gavin@cafeinternet.co.uk	8am-9pm Mon-Sat, 10am-8pm Sun	15 Pentium workstations, colour scanner & colour laser printer.	Full range of coffees, teas, soft drinks, bottled beers & wines and extensive selection of hot meals & snacks.	Internet training, independent consultancy, web design & development – available for booking. "Next generation coffee house"
Cardiff Cybercafé	Cardiff	9 Duke St. CF1 2AY T: 01222 235 760 E: pauls@cardiffcybercafe.co.uk	10am - 10pm Mon- Sun	ISP, 8 PCs, HP5 laser jet printer, scanner	Coffee, teas, pastries and cafe snacks	E-mail and web space provision/design & training. Events include art openings & game events "Friendly & Welcoming to all"
Cyberia	Edinburgh	88 Hanover St. EH2 1EL T: 0131 220 4403 E: edinburgh@cybersurf.co.uk	11am-10pm Mon-Sat, 12pm-7pm Sun.	9 PCs (486/66 & K5/90s) printers etc.	Joyfully presented hot and cold meals and snacks.	Website & gallery launches, corporate & individual training "Large, open-faced & open-minded cybercafé with an exciting menu, excellent coffee & teas & friendly staff"
Global Café	London	15 Golden Square W1 R3AG T: 0171 287 2242 W: www.pirate-radio.co.uk/global	9am-12pm Mon-Sun	10 PCs, scanner, printers, ISDN line	Teas, coffee, licensed bar, Italian style sandwiches, pastries and salads.	Private functions, regular DJ nights with live webcasts and projections, occasional art exhibitions. "Leading the Renaissance of Golden Square in Soho".
Cyberpub	Nottingham	5 Victoria Centre Parliament St. NG1 3IB T:001159 475394 E:ntm.00001@cyberpub.adr.co.uk	12pm-7pm Mon-Fri, 11.30pm-7pm, Sat, closed Sun	ISP, ISDN line, 8 terminals, printers etc.	Licensed bar, hot snacks & pub lunches.	"Queen Victoria meets Terry Gilliam"
Garland Street Café	Bury St. Edmunds	4 Garland Street, Bury St Edmunds. IT33 1E@ T: 01284 753373 ritchie@garland_cafe.dungeon.com	11am-4pm Wed-Sat, evenings 7pm-11pm, Thurs-Sun closed Mon-Tue	PC and colour printer.	Hot vegetarian dishes.	Evening performances: Soul jazz DJs-Thurs, live bands Fri & Sat, jamming session Sun.
Peak Art Cybercafé	New Mills, Peak District	30 Market St. New Mills High Peak SK22 3DS T:0166374770 E:peak@artcybercafe.cityscape.co.uk	9.30am-5pm Mon, Tues, Fri & Sat, 9.30am-2pm Wed, 9.30am-10pm Thur, 10.30-5pm Sun.	2 PCs, colour printing, b/w scanning	Hot and cold café snacks, home-made pies and soups, coffee, teas etc.	Tuition taylored to the individual's needs. Local artworks displayed, and a variety of ad hoc events.
Surf.net Café	Deptford	13 Deptford Church St. SE8 4RX T:0181 488 1200 E:surfnet@surfnet.co.uk	12pm-9pm Mon-Fri, 12pm-7pm Sat, closed Sun.	5 PCs, 1 scanner, 2 colour printers	Soft drinks or bring own alcohol, sandwiches, hot snacks, cappuccino/cocktails, teas & pastries.	Tuition available "Pleasing"
Taunton Cyber	Taunton	27 North Street TA1 ILW T: 01823 353771 E:tracey@abling.co.uk	9.30am 6pm (evenings by appointment)	4 PCs, 1 Mac, Colour printers and scanner. View Cam for CUSEEME, network games. Own servers (ABLING - ISP)	Teas, coffee, soft drinks and café snacks.	Group and individual training, web design. Also special events (home of world's first cyber-wedding) "Spacious room with modern decor & hand painted murals"
The Internet Experience	St. Neots, Cambridgeshire	11 Fishers Yard Market Square T:01480 386 836 E:gina@intecc.co.uk W:www.intecc.co.uk	9am-9pm Mon&Tue, 9am-5.30pm Wed-Fri, 10am-6pm Sat, closed Sun.	Own ISP, customers can connect own PCs to café network, 3 PCs and colour printing facilities.	Tea and coffee only.	Domain name registration, ISDN links, leased lines, virtual server, server hosting "The computer is the heart of our business"

To have your café listed please call Josephine Berry on 0171 613 4743 or email: josie@metamute.com

www.ingramcontent.com/pod-product-compliance
Lightning Source LLC
LaVergne TN
LVHW070143110826
845147LV00002B/318

* 9 7 8 1 9 0 6 4 9 6 6 1 6 *